# ESTABLISHED IN HIS RIGHTEOUSNESS

The Story of Jesus & His Bride

Joshua B. David

Established in His Righteousness

By Joshua B. David

Copyright © 2024

No part of this book may be reproduced or transmitted in any form of by any means, electronic, of mechanical, including photocopying, recording, or by any information storage and retrieval system, without the written permission from the author.

All rights reserved.

ISBN 979-8-9921067-0-1

Printed in India at www.devtechprinters.com

# Acknowledgements

First and foremost, I thank God for His grace, love, and faithfulness, which have enabled me to walk this journey and share this message of being Established in His Righteousness.

1. To my beloved wife, Mae—your unwavering support, prayers, belief, and hard work have been my anchor through the thick and thin of life. Thank you for shouldering responsibilities that allowed me the freedom to study the word of Christ and to write this book. This labor of love is as much yours as it is mine.

2. To my mother, Tryphena Barnabas David whose faithful intercession and encouragement continually inspire me to aim higher. Your prayers are a pillar in my life.

3. To my children, Jehoshaphat and John—through you, I have experienced the depth of the Father's love. You are the ones who birthed the revelation of the Father's heart in me.

4. To my spiritual daughter, Asmita Mulchandani, who labored with me tirelessly in video shooting the teachings that shaped the content of this book. Thank you for being the first to see it's potential and encouraging me to bring it to life in book form.

5. To Naomi Deola, my scribe—this dream project would not have been possible without your talent and dedication. You have truly brought this vision to life, and I am deeply grateful.

6. To my editorial team: Autumn, Samara, and Heleigh—thank you for your exceptional work in refining and shaping this book, making it accessible and impactful for my readers.

7. To Christopher Drake, for the incredible cover design that captures the essence of this book so beautifully.

8. To my Upperroom Church family—your unwavering belief, prayers, and investment in me have been invaluable. Thank you for ensuring that I lack nothing to take God's message to the world.

9. To all my Mentors and friends who believe in me and have graciously endorsed my book. Your companionship breeds confidence in me.
10. Finally, to you, my dear reader—I thank God for you. My prayer is that your life becomes a powerful testimony of being Established in His Righteousness. May His love and grace overflow in your journey. Amen!

# Endorsements

"In the grand divine exchange, God made Christ who knew no sin to be sin on our behalf, that we might have the righteousness of God in Him (2 Corinthians 5:21). Joshua David expounds on this glorious theme; addressing the fallenness of man with pastoral compassion, and faithfully pointing us to the redemptive grace of God in Christ Jesus!"

*Edmund Chan*
*Founder and Leadership Mentor,*
*Global Alliance of Intentional Disciple making Churches.*
*Singapore*

Joshua David has been one of my dear friends for over a decade. His life, leadership and wisdom has shaped my life personally and the UPPERROOM.

I am pleased to highly recommend Established In His Righteousness by Joshua David, a compelling new release from UpperRoom India. In this work, Joshua offers profound insights into our established righteousness before God through the finished work of Jesus Christ.

Joshua's approach is both thoughtful and practical, offering not just theological reflection but tangible steps for applying these teachings to daily life. Whether you are a long-time believer or just beginning to explore the Christian faith, this book provides valuable perspectives that will inspire, challenge, and encourage you on your journey.

Joshua David's voice is a needed one in the global church today. God is raising him up as a father not only to his nation but the nations of the earth.

*Michael Miller*
*Lead Pastor - Upperroom, Dallas Tx, USA*

Righteousness is the key to the kingdom of heaven; key for the unification with God; key for a nation to be exalted; key for a bonding relationship leading to peaceful coexistence toward a prosperous living ; key for hope in one's life. These truths have been beautifully interwoven in this book by Joshua David who believes and has practiced these truths. May it be a great blessing!

*Dr Paul Dhinakaran*
*Jesus Calls*

I have had the pleasure to experience the teachings in this book in several ways. First of all Pastor Joshua David led my team of leaders as well as myself through a personal teaching of the ideas and principles found here over a period of three months, allowing us to engage in question and answer time as well as conversational time to digest the rich truths that we discussed.

I was also blessed to be able to read the chapters as they came out one by one, and to process the truths therein with both Pastor Joshua and his ghost writer Naomi. This book is full of foundational insight and visionary perspective from a man who has blessed me, my family, my ministry team, and countless others across the globe, and I am convinced that everyone who reads these writings will be equally blessed. Enjoy my friends, I look forward to hearing the testimonies and of all the fruit that is sure to come!

*Pastor Ross Kellogg*
*Founder The Collective Church,*
*Washington, USA*

"Joshua David has spent decades of his life mining the truths of God's word while seeking to embody the same. In this book, he articulates immovable pillars of the Christian faith to establish the believer in a righteousness that is not fragile or based upon human effort or perception. For the days we are living in, this book is an incredible resource for those who are tired of being blown and tossed by every wind and wave of doctrine."

*Peter K. Louis*
*Founder, Braveheart Ministries. USA*


This book "Established in Righteousness " is a deep dive into the most important revelation in the New Testament. All of Paul's epistles unapologetically declares righteousness is a gift, it's by faith and we have it now not wait till you die. I thoroughly enjoyed the deep transformational truths of our righteousness in Christ that my dear friend and brother in Christ- Joshua David has presented as a true workman rightly dividing the Word of God. Brother Joshua has captured the revelation of righteousness that the church needs today to purge us from "sin consciousness " (Hebrews 10:1-3. Get ready to walk in boldness, authority and confidence as we rule and reign in this life as kings (Romans 5:17) with this " gift of righteousness " Expect answers to prayers as a way of life.

*Bro. Augie David*
*Founder, Global Leadership Alliance, USA*

Established in HIS Righteousness made me look hard at what I really believe!

Whenever I heard the word RIGHTEOUSNESS I would always think of someone doing the right thing. Like Mother Teresa or somebody who followed all the rules correctly.

I never realized that righteousness had NOTHING to do with right doing but had EVERYTHING to do with right believing.

Also that righteousness was not earned it was given!! Given? Yes a gift, as Joshua articulates. In the book of Romans the Apostle Paul speaks of RIGHTEOUSNESS as a gift. The same Apostle says in the book of Corinthians that we are the righteousness of GOD. THAT'S scandalous!! How can any human being be GOD'S righteousness. ONLY because of Jesus and the Cross! HE made us righteous. Like putting on a ROBE. Cloaked in it!

If someone asked God to show them HIS righteousness? HE would tell them to just look at those children of HIS who have believed Jesus is the Son of God who died and rose again!! THEY are MY righteousness!

Joshua David once again articulates this truth in such precision that the reader is left to make a conscious choice for themselves: Do I believe or not? He weaves this undeniable truth masterfully through chapter after chapter until the end when he says, THE GOAL IS JESUS! It all comes together!

*Mike Moore*
*Dallas Businessman*
*Author of 5 books in the Love God Series*
*IG: @mikemoore320*

"Congratulations to you Rev. Joshua David, my covenanted friend and dear Brother in the Lord Jesus". Your passionate love for GOD be it in preaching or in scripting this journal of your Journey with The Holy Spirit is pretty evident.

In these last days of growing perilous moments of hopelessness, casualness, carnality and depravity I am confident this book most definitely is a powerful tool to equip the saints to live from His righteousness.

Congratulations once again to you my dear friend!

Blessings
*Pastor Shekar Kallianpur*
*New Life Fellowship, Mumbai, India*


"Pastor Joshua is carrying vital revelation for a vital hour in history. His teachings will take your heart to a place of profound understanding. Read his books. Study his books. You will be glad you did!"

*Pastor Brad Crawford*
*Goodnews Nation*
*Forthworth, Tx, USA*


It is with great joy that I share my heartfelt endorsement for Established in His Righteousness book by my dear friend, Pastor Joshua B. David. He is not only a good friend but also a man of profound wisdom and unwavering faith. His deep understanding of the New Covenant and his passion for revealing the Father's heart is evident on every page of this book.

This is my prayer that as you dive deep into the pages of this amazing book, you'll encounter the God who not just loves but is pure love.

*Apostle Ankit Sajwan*
*FOLJ New Delhi, India*

Church alway majored on sin. The argument is when you know sin, you can walk in righteousness. But what does the Word say? "awake to righteousness and sin not".

1 Corinthians 15:34 Awake to righteousness, and sin not; for some have not the knowledge of God: I speak this to your shame. Apostle Paul never encouraged us to be awake to sin and be righteous but awake to righteousness and sin not.

We can stand in front of very high ceiling and everyone try to jump to touch the ceiling. All we can say is who jumped higher but net who touched the ceiling.

Thats exactly is man trying to reach perfection comparing one with other and all we can say is who did better but never who reached the righteousness of god? We often try to establish our own righteousness through good works, rituals, or moral behavior. However, this approach is flawed, as our self-efforts can never measure up to God's perfect standard.

Being established in righteousness means that we are firmly rooted in our identity as children of God. We are no longer defined by our past mistakes or current struggles. Instead, we are seen as righteous in God's eyes, not because of our own efforts, but because of Jesus' finished work on the cross.

Being established in righteousness has profound implications for our lives:

- Confidence before God: We can approach God with confidence, knowing that we are righteous in His eyes.
- Freedom from guilt and shame: We are no longer burdened by guilt and shame, as our sins are forgiven and forgotten.
- Boldness in prayer: We can pray with boldness, knowing that our prayers are heard and answered by a loving Father.
- Empowerment for living: We are empowered to live a life that honors God, as we are motivated by gratitude and love for Him.

This book from my son Joshua doesn't come from his knowledge of Goodness of God, His grace and His gift of righteousness but it also comes from experiencing the known truth and how it set Joshua free to serve Father without guilt or pressure to perform but enjoy being established in his righteousness.

May every reader not just know but be established permanently in the righteousness of god by faith in jesus.

*Apostle P. S. Rambabu (Rambo)*
*Holy Spirit Generation Church*
*Bangalore, India*
*www.rwo.life*

# Testimony - Naomi Deola

Writing alongside Joshua David as his scribe has been one of the greatest endeavors of my life. I feel that no one can read Joshua's words, or even speak with him, without feeling the Spirit of God emanating off of him. When I got a glimpse of chapter one of this book my entire view of the Old Testament began to change. I began to see the true design of God in all of creation and history. God began to speak to me in a way that I had never experienced before. Joshua goes to great lengths to address identity and how we see the Father, two areas where many Christians are in a battle. He reveals the simple steps to mending those broken, skewed parts. From Genesis to Revelation Joshua uncovers the heart of God and how every Christian fits into His story. I say with the greatest conviction that the Holy Spirit is resting on this book, and I am beyond grateful to have been able to work on this project firsthand. I believe that no Christian will be able to read these words without being completely transformed or compelled into rapid growth!

# Forewords

Years ago, I was listening to a Q&A session with pastors and church leaders from a variety of denominations and streams within the Church. A question was posed to the panel: What does a life of faith look like? As each leader took their turn to respond, there was a variety of answers. Some described a life marked by risk, others spoke about trust, great exploits, ministry service, or deep personal devotion and discipline. In part, these were all true aspects of how faith unfolds in the life of a believer.

The last to answer was a priest, and what he said confounded me at the time. After a pause, he responded simply, gently, and with a slight smile on his face:

"A life of faith is... relaxing."

I was entirely confused and even somewhat put off by his answer. Of all the ways to describe a life of faith, "relaxing" was certainly not on my list. But then he explained:

"A life of faith is relaxing in the way that one relaxes in the presence of a friend who they are convinced is fond of them."

When I heard this, I experienced both the tender nearness of my Father and a deep, piercing conviction by the Holy Spirit that I didn't fully believe it to be true. At that time—though I wouldn't have admitted it aloud—I believed the cross simply made me tolerable to God. Somewhere along the way, a religious spirit had settled in and deceived me, hiding from my view the extravagant, scandalous good news of the free and grace-filled gift of righteousness. In the absence of that truth, I had begun to build a life on a lie.

I was striving to prove to God that I was desirable, worthy, and useful through my own strength, self-discipline, and dead works. My so-called "life of faith" certainly wasn't relaxing; it was marked by subversive shame and endless striving. And let me tell you this: a life of striving is not a life of faith at all.

That moment inaugurated a journey of pursuit that ultimately led me to the beautiful feet of Jesus. At the foot of His cross and in view of His empty tomb, He subdued my weary soul, confronted my unbelief, and revealed the absolute sufficiency of His finished work on my behalf. He lived the perfect life that had always been just out of my reach. He suffered and died not only for me but as me. He died my death and, in turn, shared His resurrection life with me.

Christ's finished work sealed not only His triumph over sin and death but also secured my complete wholeness, holiness, and righteousness in Him. I vividly remember the moment the Spirit of adoption hit my soul. My eyes were opened to the lavish love of God, and I wept in the presence of my Father's delight. In that moment, I experienced a fullness of joy I had never known before.

I repented, turning away from a life of self-effort, and turned entirely toward Him. I placed the full weight of my dependence for life, godliness, and my future on Christ. I had been set free—not only from the lie of religion but also from myself.

There are so many beautiful gifts extended to us through the gospel of Jesus Christ. I am immensely grateful for the forgiveness of sin, union with God, provision for life, healing, wholeness, the blessed hope of His return, and unshakable peace with God. However, to me, the greatest gift of the gospel is its power to liberate me from myself. Only then could I truly discover and experience what Paul proclaimed in Galatians 2:20:

"I have been crucified with Christ. It is no longer I who live, but Christ who lives in me. The life I now live in the flesh, I live by faith in the Son of God, who loved me and gave Himself for me."

Even as I write these words, I could shout and weep in exuberant worship and overwhelming gratitude. This truth is as real for me as it was for the Apostle Paul. And if you have placed your faith in Christ, my friend, it is just as true for you.

I can think of no more transformative revelation than the free gift of righteousness in Christ. And I can think of no one more fitting to articulate and proclaim that truth than Joshua David. He not only believes it to his core, but he also lives it and points others to it in ways that have deepened my faith and immersed me in the goodness of God.

If you are hungry for deep fellowship with Jesus—if you desire a life marked by the manifest presence of God, supernatural power, and ever-growing intimacy with Him—then it begins here. The truths in the pages that follow have the power to set you free. That freedom is not just deliverance from sin, sickness, and weariness of soul, but a supernatural delivery into the delight of your Father, unbroken fellowship with the Son, and the overflowing abundance of the Spirit.

I pray with confidence that, as He did for me so many years ago, God breathes upon the words in this book. May He awaken your spirit to all that is offered to you in Jesus. May the eyes of your heart be opened to His sufficiency and your value as His prized possession and workmanship.

My prayer is that the truth Joshua shares in this book lays not only a foundation but also builds your entire life from this point forward, fully and firmly established in His righteousness alone.

*Kevin Tipps*
*Pastor Upperroom Dallas, USA*

# Content Page

| | | |
|---|---|---|
| Introduction | | 19 |
| 1 | Righteousness and the Redeemed Man | 21 |
| 2 | Righteousness and the Law | 29 |
| 3 | Righteousness and our New Husband | 38 |
| 4 | Righteousness and the Grace Covenant | 46 |
| 5 | Righteousness and Intimacy | 59 |
| 6 | Righteousness and Oneness with God | 71 |
| 7 | Righteousness and Standing Firm | 85 |
| 8 | Righteousness and Our Inheritance | 93 |
| 9 | Righteousness and the Nature of Blessings | 104 |
| 10 | Righteousness and the Provision of God | 116 |
| 11 | Righteousness and Works | 126 |
| 12 | Righteousness and the Truth of Who You Are | 138 |
| 13 | Righteousness and The blood | 147 |
| 14 | Righteousness and Judgment | 163 |

# Introduction

It was November 2, 1996. I felt the Lord's hand gently around my heart. I did not want to miss this moment; I knew I had to dig deeper into the closeness I was experiencing. I called and canceled all my plans for the evening. I remember how time seemed to escape me as I began to press in. I looked at the clock; it was 10:00pm and I continued to pray. Then it was midnight and I was still there... 1:00am... 2:00am... And then, just before 3:00am, something wondrous took place. With my physical eyes I saw a man. He wore a white robe and began to walk towards me. When I saw this man, I was overwhelmed with emotion and my eyes wept with tears. At that moment, I knew that Jesus was the one who stood in my room. I moved towards Him and began to walk with Him. Soon we came to a wall where we sat and I leaned my head against His chest; I could hear the beating of His heart. I want you to know what He said to me because it has forever changed my life, and the reason for this book. Jesus looked at me and spoke these words:

> *"My son, I love you and your sins are washed away. Your life will never be the same again. You will be the salt and the light of the world. I will put my words in your mouth and you will proclaim my gospel. I have chosen you and anointed you to mend the brokenhearted and to heal the blind eye. You are not a result of your past; you are a result of my blood, and because of my blood you are mine, completely and fully mine! Your sins no longer own you; they have no right to bind and arrest you. You do not belong to the law, you do not belong to this earth, and you do not belong to the evil one. You belong to me; you are mine!"*

In an instant I was set free. I was set free from every bondage of fear and guilt and every chain of legalism and false identity.

The Lord has made a way for you to live in absolute

freedom. So many Christians live in anxiety, depression, and under heavy burdens, even though God has promised a new and abundant life for all who believe. As you begin to study righteousness you will see that you are not called to live in lack or defeat. As you begin seeing yourself the way the Father sees you, there will be nothing left to fear; your worth and value will have a foundation that is unshakable! Creation waits with eager longing for the sons of God to be revealed. The entire world is waiting for you to step into your inheritance. Abundant life is yours, wealth and riches, freedom and prosperity, healing and true joy, power and success; these gifts are written into your birthright. My friend, I want you to know that everything you have ever needed, whether it is healing, freedom, joy, or provision, is found in Jesus, in His arms, and nowhere else.

# Chapter 1

# Righteousness and the Redeemed Man

Too often we regard the gospel as a minor steppingstone; a thing to glance at, graze on and then move past. This mindset, however, has left a gaping hole within the Bride of Christ. The Bride of Jesus, or the global church, will continue to bleed from this wound until she opens her languished eyes to see the gospel clearly. The gospel is not to be the foundation of the house that is laid and forgotten about, but rather it is to be every part of the house: the walls, the windows, the roof, and all that contributes to the experience of being *inside* the house. My prayer for you as you read this book is that your heart would be open to hearing a critical message to a sleeping Bride.

## The Fallen Man

It is crucial that we grasp how destitute the human race became through one act. When Adam sinned the entire world was affected. Sin entered and death was the result. Death cast its shadow over all humanity, because all have sinned. Through one man's sin every person and every part of creation had fallen. The gravity of sin has rippled throughout humanity from the beginning of time into this very moment. The sin of Adam has left no man untouched.

It is important to understand the nature of sin. When God created Adam and Eve there was nothing missing, nothing broken, nothing flawed. The first two people to walk the earth experienced perfect and unhindered fellowship with God. This relationship was pure. They spoke, walked, met, and communed with Him side by side. God's original design was to be in complete and ongoing relationship with us. God made known to Adam that if he disobeyed and ate from the tree of the knowledge of good and evil he would surely die. The Lord made everything quite simple: there is life in God and death in sin. "Of the tree of the knowledge of good and evil you shall not eat," (Genesis 2:17 NKJV) said the voice of the Lord.

There was another voice, however; a convincing, malicious and manipulative voice. This voice came out of the belly of Satan who wore the skin of a serpent. "You will not certainly die…for God knows that when you eat from it your eyes will be opened, and you will be like God, knowing good and evil" (Genesis 3:4-5 NIV). Adam then submitted to the evil one, and listened to the words of a foreign tongue. In a moment sin entered the world for the first time, along with sickness, curses, abuse, greed, and every kind of evil. The pure life and the perfect relationship with the Lord was gone. All of creation plummeted into the merciless clutches of darkness. The Lord spoke truly in saying "You will surely die," for in the very moment that Adam sinned, he died.

Picture a phone in your imagination. A phone needs a battery to live, storage and programs to hold memories and function, and a sim card for connection. Imagine the battery will represent our physical, human body, the storage and programs are our soul, and the sim card as our eternal spirit.

The battery supplies power to the phone much like the physical body keeps us alive. Our body is a mere vehicle keeping us usable on this earth. When the body dies, much like the battery, we are of no use. David made this clear in his cry to the Lord, "In the grave I cannot praise you". (Psalms 6:5, 30:9) Even King Hezekiah said the same thing in Isaiah 38:18. The moment Adam committed the first sin it was not his body that died. We know this because he lived for many years and had many children.

The soul is what makes sense of it all. It holds all the data as the storage and programs of a phone would. The soul is what gives us the ability to experience emotions and gather significance through memories and thought. The moment Adam committed the first sin it was not his soul that died. We know this because he was still able to think, feel and imagine; he was still able to reason and consider.

It was in the moment Adam committed the first sin that his spirit died. A sim card possesses the function of connection by connecting with and catching a tower's signals, just as the spirit does with us and God. The sim card fried the day Adam sinned. Jesus tells us that He is the life (John 14:6); therefore, when Jesus withdrew from Adam's spirit, his spirit died, for the absence of life is death. Death first took its hold of the spirit, but slowly it spread to the soul and subsequently into the physical realm, covering the body until death is now a common and expected occurrence, tarnishing God's perfect plan and original design.

One sin infected creation and left it with a terrible groan for help and a question that needed an answer… "who will save us?" A search for this answer began. Every human was now born a sinner and was destined to death, curses and a life of misery. Every human was now sentenced to hell from birth. The human condition was utterly hopeless. Our heritage became that of eternal damnation, not because of what we did but because of what Adam did. Something in man was starving, starving for the connection to God that had been lost in the fall. Something in man was dying, dying from the lack of God within him. Desperate to reconnect with God, men began to work with all their strength, using everything in their soul. People began worshiping nature, or the universe, or even their own imaginations. This was the introduction to religion.

Religious acts are nothing more than futile attempts to reconnect to God. If we again recall the phone analogy we can see that the battery, storage, and programs in the phone were never meant to catch the signals of the tower. This is the role of the sim card. The body and soul keep us alive and bring significance, but the connection factor is left to our spirit who died the day sin entered the world. Mankind strived desperately, but every attempt was rooted in fleshly need and prideful gain. Man began to invent idols, worshiping and serving himself and what was evil. Man invented religions of every kind, aspiring to justify

> **Religious acts are nothing more than futile attempts to reconnect to God**

himself through works and actions. God then saw that every attempt made by mankind to reconnect with Him was only leading to further corruption, worsening the already miserable condition of the human race. How did God tell the world that every attempt at reconnection was an act of sin? He introduced the law.

## The Law

Before the law came to be, sin was present, however, sin was not yet identified. Through the law there is knowledge of sin. "What then shall we say? That the law is sin? By no means! Yet if it had not been for the law, I would not have known sin" (Romans 7:7 ESV). This passage gives us a clear explanation for why the law was given to us by God. The law was rendered to us to expose our sin and reveal that man cannot come back to God on his own. Man cannot revive his own spirit. For instance, in Exodus 32 the Israelites crafted a golden calf in an effort to fulfill themselves and the Lord gave them the law through Moses saying "you shall not worship any image made by (human) hands" (Exodus 20:4-5). This was not the Lord's judgment, this was instead His vital diagnosis. We have come to the crossroad where many have been led astray - they have mistook the diagnosis as a prescription, or way of treatment! God gave us the law as a flashlight to shine on ourselves and help us realize that there was darkness; that we were darkness. He did not give it to us as the light of the world.

> The law was rendered to us to expose our sin and reveal that man cannot come back to God on his own.

I have often described the law as a diagnostic machine, for this is the very purpose of the law, to diagnose. Once again, there is always another voice, a cunning and crafty voice, the voice of Satan. This deceptive voice takes the law, much like he did the forbidden fruit, and says "If you do this you will be like God. If you put your trust in the law and if you do the righteous acts, only then will you be restored... just don't make any mistakes." Mankind, frantic and doomed, clings to an artificial promise, but "no man is justified by the keeping of the law" (Galatians 2:16). So a treacherous lie begins to spread slowly, that the law would bring salvation. We are told in Isaiah 64:6 (NIV), however, that "all our righteous acts are like filthy rags." There is a common ideology that believes if someone is "good" then they are righteous in the sight of God. Please realize something extremely urgent here - our good works are primarily a result of the forbidden fruit that Adam ate. Did God tell Adam to refrain from eating of the fruit of the knowledge of evil? Yes; however, that statement would be incomplete, for the fruit did not only possess the knowledge of evil but also the knowledge of good. Let me put it very simply...every "good" in our culture, in our instincts, in the world around us, cannot be our justification because it, too, is a result of the fall of creation. In our flesh nothing good dwells. This is why Paul says "Where then is boasting? It has been excluded. By what kind of law? Of works? No, but by a law of faith" (Romans 3:27 NASB). If we were to boast in good works and in our practice of the law, would we not simply be boasting about our own sin and identification of it? Would we not only be boasting of another failed attempt to once again reach God? The law was never meant to save us. The law was to reveal to man that it is impossible to reach God on our own with a dead spirit. The law was given to us to answer creation's cry of "who will save us?" by simply pointing to one Man...the righteous Man.

## The Righteous Man

By one man did sin enter and by one man so did salvation. "For the law was given through Moses; grace and truth came through Jesus Christ" (John 1:17 ESV). The previous sections were focused primarily on the state of humanity before the revealing of the Savior. This was to put an emphasis on the despairing and desperate condition of life devoid of God and our connection to Him. This was to describe the cavernous darkness in order that the light would be found and treasured.

In Jeremiah 23:6 (ESV) we read that "In his days Judah will be saved, and Israel will dwell securely. And this is the name by which he will be called: 'The LORD is our righteousness.'" Let us pay close attention to the wording in this passage. We are told that it will be "in His days." Jeremiah is careful and clear in his diction. Not in "their" days, not in "my" days, not even in "your" days, but in "*HIS*" days. In doing this, Jeremiah takes all eyes off of you and me and tells us to cast our gaze onto Him, the righteous Man. In the days of the righteous Man, or in the days of Jesus Christ, Jeremiah is heralding "pay attention! Something great will happen. The Lord will become our righteousness! My own works will not become my righteousness, nor will it be the law, it is the Lord who will become my righteousness."

The word Immanuel means "God with us" and often I hear many accept this as the truth while twisting it into their own image. God with us... as we walk righteously. God with us... when we feel Him. God with us... but still part of Him is far off. These are lies that must be addressed immediately. In 1 Corinthians 1:30 (ESV) we are told "because of him you are in Christ Jesus, who became to us wisdom from God, righteousness and sanctification and redemption." This means that the unattainable requirement given by God through the law was met, filled, and final in Christ. The Lord is my wisdom, my righteousness, my sanctification, and my redemption. Everything stolen from me because of sin and every diagnosis from the law is made right and fulfilled in Jesus Christ.

He has become my new identity. This is why Jesus said "as in the wilderness Moses lifted up a brazen serpent and everyone who looked at the serpent was saved, so shall the son of man be lifted up and all who look at Him will be saved" (John 3:14). There is a simplicity in this that we must take hold of if we are to truly walk in the identity that the Lord has bought for us. Romans 5:19 (NLT) says, "Because one person disobeyed God, many became sinners. But because one other person obeyed God, many will be made righteous." I have often wondered why it is that so many can easily accept that because of Adam's disobedience we have become sinners, but so many find it immensely difficult to believe that because of Jesus' obedience we have become righteous. The answer to this question I have found to be somewhat simple. If we are looking at ourselves we are putting ourselves in the position of Jesus and therefore hoping to be our own justification. We see closely our sin and filth and cannot fathom being made clean… but we are told that whoever looks to Him will be made righteous. You are not a part of the equation of being right with God, nor are you a part of the process. My friend, you are the product! The moment I began to understand that my righteousness is a result of His doing, not my doing; His believing, not my believing; His obedience, not my obedience, the accusations of the enemy were silenced forever! This is a great revelation for when you fall prey to sin, when you make mistakes, or when the devil comes to you claiming that you are no longer a child of God because of your failure. From here you can proudly proclaim that it was never you who gained this sonship or this righteousness in the first place! It wasn't because of anything you have done! You can now declare that everything you have is because of Jesus and what He has accomplished. The sonship you have gained was completely at His expense and you are now a participant of His finished work! Paul tells us that "it is through faith that a righteous person has life" (Romans 1:17 NLT) and that "Christ is the culmination of the law so that there may be righteousness for everyone who believes" (Romans 10:4 NIV). Christ is the end of the law. Our Lord has made a simple way home and by faith in Him alone do we now become righteous.

> The moment I began to understand that my righteousness is a result of His doing, not my doing; His believing, not my believing; His obedience, not my obedience, the accusations of the enemy were silenced forever!

Let us cast off the yoke of sin and despair, for we see that the law has exposed how the sin of Adam was great and although it severed our connection to God by plaguing us with dead spirits, the righteousness of Jesus Christ was far greater. Jesus, by His life and death has resurrected our spirits and become the fulfillment of the law and the Savior of the world. The Lord has become our righteousness.

# Chapter 2

# Righteousness and the Law

There are certain ideologies and strongholds that must be abolished as you begin to walk in the identity offered by the savior. You will begin to discover very soon that in order to live a life of freedom, you must unlearn the damaging habits that you may have become accustomed to. You must come out from under the yoke that you may have accepted long ago. An interesting thing about freedom is that it can only be offered; there is no one who can force you to walk in it because that would not be freedom at all. Your freedom has been offered and now it is up to you to grab ahold of it! As you begin to claim freedom as your own and come out from under the stronghold of the law, there are many blessings that will follow.

## The Stronghold of the Law

In chapter one we laid a foundation to build upon. You should now be familiar with the first entrance of sin through Adam and the devastation that followed this event. We covered the reason and purpose of why the law was given; a diagnosis that is often mistaken as a prescription. In the last chapter we left off with the life and sacrifice of Jesus Christ. His victory! His grace! His very righteousness, which has become our own! With definitions and knowledge much is built, but only when it is paired with action and application will it be of any worth. It is not enough to know this in theory. Only through action and application with this truth can one be benefited.

It is now time to answer a question that will, or maybe already has, surface in your mind. How is one able to break the stronghold of the law? But first, what is a stronghold? It is common to falsely define a concept and in doing so, give it more power than it deserves. A stronghold is merely a belief system that you have formed in your mind through experiences you have had, content you have consumed, and a worldview in which you have been taught. Such things (experiences, content, teachings, etc.) create a lens in which you see the world, and more importantly, a lens in which you see God. When considering the story of Job, we clearly see that it is Satan who is causing the distress and turmoil in his life, and yet Job, creating from his experience a broken lens, decided that it is God. Our lens is very important; it dictates how we process everything that we encounter. People can experience the same occurrence and still, based on their lens, be impacted in very different ways. Take for example a police officer. Without the officer changing anything about his appearance, he will evoke very different responses from those around him. When a criminal sees a cop he sees an enemy, something which he must run from and fear. While the son of the officer sees someone who he can run *to*, someone he loves, and someone who loves him! It is crucial to understand that different lenses formulate your entire approach to life, and a skewed lens of God can cause many painful troubles.

When your lens of God becomes skewed it can open the door to a spirit of offense. The spirit of offense is something that must be addressed in order to be avoided. Offense plagues those who are under the yoke of the law, and should not be a thing that has power over those living in the covenant of grace. I would like to bring to your mind a message spoken by Jesus, this was a very controversial message, so controversial in fact that many left the Lord when they heard His words that day. Jesus was speaking in the synagogue, so keep in mind what kind of audience He was speaking to. The synagogue was a place filled with Jewish elites and scholars. Jesus, to a crowd of intentional and diligent students of the Old Testament, explains that His flesh is bread and anyone who eats His flesh will never

> Offense plagues those who are under the yoke of the law, and should not be a thing that has power over those living in the covenant of grace.

die, and those who drink His blood will have life. Those who heard Jesus' words that day were confronted with a decision, for the law says that one *shall not drink blood.*

Now, if you examine this situation very carefully, you will find that there is somewhat of an order that detains those who have a stronghold of the law. First, their lens of God was twisted; they began to see Him as a heretic because His teaching upset their preconceived ideas and worldviews. Second, the spirit of offense was given an opportunity to enter. The disciples were in close relationship with Jesus and even *they* began to complain out of confusion. The offense that was growing in this specific situation stemmed from the assumption of the people; they had a certain idea of what Jesus should look like, what He should teach like, and how He should fit into their lives.

In Second Kings chapter 5, the prophet Elisha is approached by Naaman, the commander of the king of Syria's army, as a great and honourable man who was also a leper, who wanted to be healed of leprosy, So prophet Elisha tells Naaman to wash himself seven times in the river and then he would be restored to full health. However, the reaction from the commander is absurd, as he becomes very angry and disconcerted. Why? Why would this commander be upset when he is about to receive his healing? The scripture explains that Naaman had expected Elisha to come to him, make a sacrifice, call on the name of the Lord, and lay his hands on him! Naaman was blinded by his conjectures and he missed the glory of what God was doing because of offense.

A skewed perception of the Lord becomes a breeding ground for offense. When Jesus had spoken such a controversial teaching many submitted to the spirit of offense and allowed the law to become to them a stumbling block. However, what they

> Under the law you will believe what you understand, but in perfect grace you believe first and then the understanding will come after.

did not see is that Jesus was leading them into a new depth of faith. Under the law you will believe what you understand, but in perfect grace you believe *first* and then the understanding will come after.

The disciples are a perfect example of what it is to believe first! When Jesus saw many leave, He turned to ask His disciples if they were planning to leave with the others. Through the confusion, fear, and trial, the disciples made the simplest, yet most paramount decision that they could have in that moment, and that was to believe! In John 6:68 (NIV) Peter responds with a question saying "to whom shall we go? You have the words of life." Peter did not yet understand that Jesus Himself *was* the life, nor did he fully understand what Jesus meant when He said that His flesh and blood are the *eternal* life. Peter, however, made the decision to believe first and in doing so began to step out from under the yoke of the law. If you look at the fruit that followed this decision, it is priceless! Jesus did mighty works with and through the disciples, their lives and every life to follow was changed forever, and all because they chose to resist offense, and they chose to believe!

> Peter, however, made the decision to believe first and in doing so began to step out from under the yoke of the law.

As you begin to walk in your identity, you must clean the lens in which you see God in order to see Him rightly; you must make no allowances for the spirit of offense, and you must believe; you must believe first!

### Curses and Blessings

It is human nature to be fixated on ourselves, our joys and pains as well as our mistakes and failures. This is one of the reasons that humans fall under the yoke of the law so easily. When you become fixated on the greatness of your sin, you will also become fixated on the greatness of your works. You will begin to believe that it is by your works that you are free, by your works that you are loved, and that it is by your works that you have been saved. In John chapter six, however, a crowd brings a certain, interesting question before the Lord. *"What shall we do, that we might work the works of God?"* (John 6:28 KJV) Those who are asking this question have lived in a culture where the law was well known and strictly observed.

If you take a moment to observe the question, you will notice that those who are asking are still stuck under the yoke of the law and are seeking a work or an action in order to please God. Jesus had come to a culture in which the law had been idolized. Most of the men in that time and land had been versed and studied in the passages and beliefs of the Torah since the age of twelve. Jesus had come to such a culture in order to reveal the truth and break off the chains of our futile works. With one simple answer does Jesus free us of our obligation to the law. *"This is the work of God, that you believe in Him whom He has sent" (John 6:29 ESV)*. When Jesus is asked what work one must do in order to please God, His answer is simply *believe!* Jesus turns their eyes from their works to His salvation and His grace! A concept like this would be extremely difficult for those who had known the law so well to grasp.

Throughout the Old Testament we see God raising up judges, kings, and prophets to deal with the external troubles such as fighting battles, freeing slaves, and preserving that which is on the outside. Jesus was the first to even have access to the inside! Under the law you live in a world of "ifs." *If* you make a sacrifice then you will receive forgiveness or, *if* you can reach this standard then you will be righteous. This is what the law teaches. For example, in Deuteronomy 28:1-2 we are told,

> *"Now it shall come to pass, if you diligently obey the voice of the Lord your God, to observe carefully all His commandments which I command you today, that the Lord your God will set you high above all nations*

> *of the earth. And all these blessings shall come upon you and overtake you, because you obey the voice of the Lord your God..." (Deuteronomy 28:1-2 NKJV)*

As you continue to read the chapter you will see that every blessing in this passage is based on obedience and something that you have to offer.

Another thing that you will become aware of as you read, is that the list of curses is three times longer than the list of blessings. Disobedience revokes every blessing into a curse; a horrible curse! Many New Testament believers still choose to live in subjection to the fear of such curses. This belief, however, still resides under a mindset of "ifs" and Jesus has come to replace the "if" with "because!" Because He was punished for your blessings, chastised for your peace, wounded for your healing, and has paid the debt of your sin, you have been uprooted from the lineage of Adam and inserted into the royal blood of Christ! The Lord your God has taken every curse when He hung on that tree, and because of Him you are blessed!

Now, one of the Old Covenant curses for disobedience is a curse of barrenness, while another is the curse of an uprooted tent and the loss of freedom. In Isaiah 54 we are relieved of the shame and pain of barrenness and slavery.

> *"Sing, O barren one, you who have not borne! Break forth into singing, and cry aloud, you who have not labored with child! For more are the children of the desolate, than the children of the married woman, says the Lord. Enlarge the place of your tent, and let them stretch out the curtains of your dwellings; do not spare; lengthen your cords, and strengthen your stakes. For you shall expand to the right and to the left, and your descendants will inherit the nations, and make the desolate cities inhabited. 'Do not fear, for you will not be ashamed; neither be disgraced, for you will not be put to shame; for you will forget*

*the shame of your youth, and will not remember the reproach of your widowhood anymore. For your Maker is your husband, the Lord of hosts is His name; and your Redeemer is the Holy One of Israel; He is called the God of the whole earth. For the Lord has called you like a woman forsaken and grieved in spirit, like a youthful wife when you were refused, says your God. For a mere moment I have forsaken you, but with great mercies I will gather you. With a little wrath I hid My face from you for a moment; but with everlasting kindness I will have mercy on you.' Says the Lord, your Redeemer. For this is like the waters of Noah to Me; for as I have sworn that the waters of Noah would no longer cover the earth, so have I sworn that I would not be angry with you, nor rebuke you." (Isaiah 54:1-9 NKJV)*

In the passage from Deuteronomy 28 every blessing is based on your obedience. In the passage from Isaiah 54 the blessings are unconditional. You can now begin to turn your mindset from *if* to *because*! Every blessing in Isaiah 54 is now yours due to Isaiah 53 where we are told that *God has laid on Him the iniquity of us all*. In this you must know that the curses for your disobedience are not yours to bear. We are told in Galatians that Christ has rescued us from the curse pronounced by the law. Jesus has taken the consequences from your past, future, and present, and in return handed you every blessing from God.

Please understand and remember that you are fully blessed by the King, Jesus Christ! This is why Paul asked the question, "Since he did not spare even his own Son but gave him up for us all, won't he also give us everything else?" (Romans 8:32 NLT). You have already been blessed! The only way curses can be applied to your life is if you willfully put yourself under its yoke. You *must* learn to walk in your freedom! Jesus never fasted and prayed to be blessed or to be filled with the Holy Spirit; instead, He did it because He *was* blessed and He *was* filled with the Holy Spirit! We see this when Jesus goes to the river Jordan to be baptized. Upon Jesus the Spirit descended like a dove, and it was after this that the Spirit of the Lord led Him to the wilderness where He fasted and prayed. Under the yoke of the Law you are told that *if* you fast and pray, *if* you work and strive, only then, will you be worthy of blessings. In Christ Jesus everything changes! You must understand that it is *because* of Jesus that you are fully and completely blessed and filled with the Spirit of the Lord. Everything you do for Christ *must* be a reaction to His endless blessings and affections for you, or else it is only an empty attempt to gain that which you already have!

> Everything you do for Christ must be a reaction to His endless blessings and affections for you, or else it is only an empty attempt to gain that which you already have!

## Verdict

We are born into a world that sin has tainted and we often let our skewed lenses and broken perspectives be the driving force in our evaluations. We often forget that the Lord our God is the God of redemption! When sin first entered our world the curse came upon it. In Genesis 3 we hear God said, *"'Cursed is the ground because of you; through painful toil you will eat food from it all the days of your life. It will produce thorns and thistles for you...'"* (Genesis 3:17-18 NIV). In Isaiah 55:13 (NLT) we are told of our savior and His great restoration when it says, *"Where once there were thorns, cypress trees will grow. Where nettles grew, myrtles will sprout up. These events will bring great honor to the Lord's name; they will be an everlasting sign of his power and love."* What was once cursed is now blessed, and God does not withhold anything good from you!

Like Israel we have a choice today to choose between blessings and curses. We can either choose the curses by putting confidence in our own works or choose the blessings by putting confidence in Jesus' finished works on the cross. I want you to know that Jesus is holding out His hand to you. He is waiting on the path of freedom and all you must do is believe; believe first and everything else will follow.

# Chapter 3

# Righteousness and our New Husband

God does not do anything without intention; we see this in all of creation. Trees are not only beautiful, they are also created to produce oxygen. The sun does not only give light, but also warmth. Even something as seemingly insignificant as a worm has a purpose. God is a God of intentionality. There is a reason behind everything that He has done, everything that He will do, and everything that He is doing now. When Jesus came to earth it was not to reveal His power and it was not to gain respect or get revenge on the enemy. Jesus came to the earth for *you* as the Messiah and perfect savior. He ascended for you and I as a perfect high priest, and soon He will be coming back for us as our bride groom. You, my friend, are simply His reason; you are His goal.

> Jesus came to the earth for you as the High Priest and perfect husband.

## The High Priest

Certainly our Lord came to earth as our Savior but when He arose, He arose as our High Priest forever! A High Priest is the person chosen by God Himself to represent His people to Him, and Him to His people. He is the mediator between God and man. Jesus Christ wasn't gifted to us as a great prophet, for a prophet is from God to man, The Lord was given to us as the great High Priest. The Lord was very intentional with this; every high priest must be taken from the children of man. God could not manufacture for us a high priest in heaven because this priest *must* be found here on earth. When Jesus came, He did not only die for you, but He now lives for you as well! In Exodus 28 we are informed that it is *because of Him that we are accepted.* You do not live a certain way to receive His presence, for it is indeed *by* His presence that you *can* live a certain way, in the way of holiness! If you were able through your works to be holy then there would be no need for the great sacrifice of Jesus Christ as we are told in scripture. Hebrews 7:11 (TPT) says, *"If any of the Levitical priests who served under the law had the power to bring us to perfection, then why did God send Christ as priest after the likeness of Melchizedek?"*

The law is similar to an X-ray machine. The purpose of such a machine is to identify what is broken or contaminated. However, if someone were to get an X-ray weekly and expect this to cure his or her disease this would be quite absurd! All that an X-ray can do is identify the condition, after that you must receive treatment and true medicine! My friend, the medicine has arrived and the disease of sin has lost its power. In Hebrews 7 it is made known to us that the strength of sin is in the law but as you continue to study this chapter you will also be told that it is the High priest who strengthens the *law*! The high priest has the ultimate authority! Without the high Priest the Law would be meaningless as there would be no authority to execute it. Even in the days of old the High Priest was the one who had the final say, it was the High Priest who could cast a leper out of the community! So if our High Priest has been given the final say and the ultimate authority, if He has made a new law and written a new covenant then why is it that we still continue to live in fear of falling short? The answer to this question is really quite simple. Our human nature urges us to base our view and make our calculations off of our *feelings*. When you do something inherently good, you may feel righteous, and it is easy to let your feelings deceive you into believing that good works are what make you righteous. When you do something wrong or make a mistake, you may feel unworthy, and again, your feelings can trick you into thinking that your own acts, good or bad, are your identity. You must learn to walk forth in confidence of Christ (It is the confidence in which Christ walked when He was on the planet Earth) Jesus demonstrated us what permanent sonship looks like despite what your feelings say. The kingdom of God was not established on *feelings*, but on the *truth!* Everyday you will begin to learn that your true identity is not in everything that you feel, but in *everything* that He is! His truth is far greater than our feelings!

God sent to us a new and different rank of priest! *New* is such a beautiful word. When you hear that the Lord did something *new*, it means He did something that had never been done before. Aaron was a high priest of the old covenant but this old covenant had no power to cure us of our sin and darkness, so God brought to us a *new* Covenant and a *new* High Priest!

The first thing that Jesus did when He became High Priest was He replaced the law. We are told in the scripture that it was necessary to change the law since the high priest was changed. You are no longer bound by the old law. How can you receive a speeding ticket if there is no speed limit? In the book of Zachariah we are told of a story about a high priest whose name was Joshua. It is described to us that the high priest, Joshua, stood with filthy garments and the devil stood at his right hand. In this picture it seems that the enemy has the right to accuse Joshua who is clothed in that which is filthy, but instead the Lord rebukes Satan and He clothes Joshua with pure vestments! What a beautiful picture of what Jesus has done for us. The story is prophesying that the law will be changed and your accuser will no longer have the right to speak a word against you! The Lord is saying that the law that came on Mount Sinai will no longer govern the heavens, but the new law that has now been established on Calvary is what governs them! Jesus said Himself of the law, *"I have not come to abolish them but to fulfill them"* (Matthew 5:17 ESV), and once it is fulfilled there is no more use of it. So we have been given a new covenant; a better covenant and this happened the moment that Jesus took His rightful place as High Priest.

The Lord forged a way for you. He cut down the trees, uprooted the stumps, and tilled the ground into a soft trail. God has made a perfect way, and yet many still choose to walk on an unclear path. Believers are still trudging a trail overcome with thorns and hidden rocks.

One day during lent some of my friends came over for dinner. Many of them were Christians and were observing lent by fasting and praying, some were not eating certain foods and only wore white clothing during this time. As we began to have a discussion around the table it was very evident that many of them did not really understand the freedom Jesus brought us by His ultimate sacrifice. They confessed Jesus as their Lord and Savior but were still bound by laws and thought they needed to be justified before God by their works. That night my brother, Moses, and I had a long discussion about how we could help our friends to see the truth. They are in bondage when what really belongs to them is freedom. A few days later my brother came to me with a picture of Jesus. In this picture Jesus was on the cross, but He was not hanging, He was sitting; He was pondering. I asked my brother what this picture could mean and He responded, *"Jesus is wondering. What more can I do for them?"* You see, it was *Him* who replaced the law! It was *Him* who created a better way at such a great cost! But it is *us* who decided to cling to the law; it was *us* who memorized and idolized its empty tasks. So let us remember, the veil has been torn, the new High Priest has been sworn in, and we are exempt from the charges of the law! The great High Priest has established a new way, a better way!

As you begin to understand this you will discover that everything is found in Him. When you are afraid you will find a hiding place in Him, when you are broken you will find a hospital in Him, and when you are in need you will find every answer, solution, fulfillment, desire, and true nourishment in His very hand! Jesus, as the great High Priest, has become your justification; He is your representative. As David's victory over Goliath reflected and constituted all of Israel, Jesus' life, death, resurrection, and every victory in between has become your garment!

**The New Husband**

It is time to study something magnificent! In Romans 7:1-6, Paul writes to those who are familiar with the law. In doing so, his audience becomes everyone. Paul is addressing everyone! Paul, in the form of a question, relates the covenant of the law to a covenant of marriage. He explains that when a man dies his wife is no longer bound to him saying, *"Don't you know that when a person dies it ends his obligation to the law?"* (Romans 7:1 TPT). He is explaining that the law is powerless after death. *When a person dies, it is the end.* For example, a married couple is bound by the law to remain together until separated by death, but when one spouse dies, the other is released from the law of marriage. So then if a wife is joined to another man while married, she commits adultery, but if her husband dies, she is obviously free from the marriage contract and may marry another man without being judged. This very same principle applies to your relationship with God. Now, it is important that you recognize that you have been crucified with Christ and in doing so, you have died to your first husband, *the law,* and you are free to marry another. Notice how I have stated that *you are free* to marry another. In the last chapter I mentioned the dichotomy of freedom and how it can only be offered, but it is up to the individual to step into their own freedom. This is often where fear tries to slip in, and frequently a great longing for freedom is replaced with a terror of marriage to another.

> you have been crucified with Christ and in doing so, you have died to your first husband, the law, and you are free to marry another.

The first husband made a practice of revealing to the bride her shortcomings and failures. The first husband accused and belittled her. When the law first came, we were merely living natural lives and it was the law, the first husband who actually began to awaken in us a sinful desire. We are told in Hebrews 7:5 that the sinful desire in you is rooted in your belief in the law, which is your old husband. As you take off the weights of the law and step into the new covenant the Lord begins to fill you with a new and pure desire that comes from Him, the new husband! It was the old husband who made the bride believe that she was barren, because the fruit of the law and devotion *to the law is the fruit of death*. The bride lived in misery with her first husband since the power of the law is accusations and the fruit of the law is death. From the wounds and pain, trepidation was birthed! When the bride was rescued, she began to run, maybe without even noticing that she was running from her rescuer!

Now, with the old husband you were unable to become pregnant or bear fruit because the old husband could only see your darkness, he could only identify your faults. He couldn't help you. If you desire to bear fruit it is essential that you first detach completely from the old husband. Secondly, if you desire to bear fruit, you must remarry! Can a woman conceive a child on her own? Of course not! Although the old husband would not allow you to bear fruit, there is great news... The new husband is different!

The new husband is gentle and humble in heart. He is patient and overflowing with perfect grace! The new husband is nothing like the old, and you cannot look to what is failed and dead as an example if you are going to succeed in what is new! You cannot look to the law to get closer to God. You are free of the old husband, it is time to leave behind the guilt and pain of that relationship, and it is time to walk boldly and freely into a New Covenant of grace and love with a perfect husband. In this New Covenant the Lord has created for you a resting place and in it is fullness of joy and peace, unconditional love, and a pure intimacy from which you will bear much fruit!

**The Resting Place**

He is calling you into His rest. There is a gentle yet earnest call from the Lord, He is saying *come away with me*. My friend, I would like you to become aware of a calling that is over your life - you have been called to be a resting place for God! In *you* is where God desires to dwell, it is where He longs to abide. You cannot, however, be a resting place for the Lord until you find rest in *Him*. Would a parent find rest when their child is sick? Would a husband find peace when his wife is in distress? Can our God find rest in us when we are sick with sin and striving in vain works? The Lord *cannot* find rest in you until you find rest in Him, but I would like you to understand something that I hope will fill you with peace. The Lord is easy to find rest in! For example, as you begin to see Him clearly, you will learn that He is not capricious or angry, but rather, He is *slow* to anger and abounding in steadfast love! This revelation may cause your spirit to sigh in relief. As you look even deeper into Him, you will begin to feel the gravity of His sacrifice. He lived a perfect life and died a brutal death to save you, and he rose as the High Priest to defend you! Over your soul a peace will fall as you wonder at this beautiful fact. Finally, as you draw closer and closer, fear will begin to fall away and you will smile to know that He is already pleased with you. He has already blessed you, and there is freedom in His arms! Before you know it, you will begin to enjoy the ultimate comfort, you will begin to find rest as you walk to Him and as you see Him clearly, and in turn, He will find rest in you!

There is an intimacy in this revelation of Christ. Once you begin to see Him as your ultimate Bridegroom and the High Priest you will experience closeness that the Law could never provide. From this you will bear fruit; fruits of life, joy, peace, love, wisdom, strength and every good thing! God is calling us to such a simple and perfect relationship with Him, and He is restoring to us what had been lost and destroyed in the garden. His call is very gentle and very earnest - *come away with me.*

> Once you begin to see Him as your ultimate Bridegroom and the High Priest you will experience closeness that the Law could never provide.

It is amazing once we begin to realize how entangled our soul can be with the law. Even when one has been born again, there are still certain habits that *must* be broken! There is so much rest that comes with every fresh revelation of the Lord. So much peace fills those who know that there is no end to this New Covenant of grace!

## Verdict

Our High Priest permanently holds the priestly office and His reign will never end, He will never fail! You are free to let go of the lifeless clasp of the old covenant and take hold of the everlasting, never failing, perfect hand of God. You are free to step into a new covenant. The old husband only bore you death and pain but the Lord has much in store for you, and in Him you will bear the fruit of true and abundant life! The Lord has taken off your filthy garments as He did with Joshua the High Priest. You are a *new* creation, and when God uses the word *new* it truly means *new*! Now you no longer have to live as who you have been, what you have done, or the feelings you feel, but instead you are free to live in who *He* is, what *He* has done, and in the truth of *His* words!

God has become your husband. He is your representative, your great High Priest, and He has broken off the chains of religion, disarmed the accusations of the law and has handed you His every victory, His every blessing, and His very righteousness as a garment to cover you! *"Now if anyone is enfolded into Christ, he has become entirely new. All that was related to the old order has vanished. Behold, everything is fresh and new" (2 Corinthians 5:17 TPT)*. This has been prophesied of us since the days of old as the prophecy from the book of Isaiah declares, *"I am doing something brand new, unheard of. Even now it sprouts and grows and matures. Don't you perceive it? I will make a way in the wilderness and open up flowing streams in the desert" (Isaiah 43:19 TPT)*.

God is a God of intention, and He has intentionally created something new for you and I. The new husband is nothing like that of the old, the new covenant nothing like that of the past, and behold the new has come!

## Chapter 4

# Righteousness and the Grace Covenant

I believe that you will experience a great freedom as you continue to understand the depth of the *Grace Covenant* that the Lord has created you for. As you walk in such freedom there will be no struggle within your heart and the accusations from the enemy, from the law, and from your own conscience will be silenced. You will be established, rooted, and grounded in the reality of what Christ has done!

In Exodus 28:36-38 (ESV) it is written,

> *"You shall make a plate of pure gold and engrave on it, like the engraving of a signet, 'Holy to the Lord.' And you shall fasten it on the turban by a cord of blue. It shall be on the front of the turban. It shall be on Aaron's forehead, and Aaron shall bear any guilt from the holy things that the people of Israel consecrate as their holy gifts. It shall regularly be on his forehead, that they may be accepted before the Lord."*

In this we see that Aaron, as the high priest, is the mediator between God and the people. The gold plate, which Aaron was to wear on His forehead permanently, is engraved with the words *Holy unto the Lord.* This was so that God would accept Israel. The problem with this system is that it has to be repeated over and over. Although Aaron wore the words *Holy unto God,* Aaron was merely a man and mankind is prone to faults and failures. This system could only be a temporary reflection of that which is eternal! When Jesus became our High priest, we became accepted solely because of Him, His righteousness, His holiness, and His purity - not our own. It is only after you grasp this that you will be prepared to defend against the accusing voices that rise to condemn.

# The Voice of the Enemy

There are three primary accusers, and the first of the three is the devil himself.

The voice of Satan enters through our mind and twists our imagination to work against us! The Bible says in 2 Corinthians 10:5 (NKJV) that we are to cast down *"imaginations, and every high thing that exalteth itself against the knowledge of God, and bringing into captivity every thought to the obedience of Christ."* Here we are being taught to take hold of our mind and thoughts and place them under the authority of the Lord. It is impossible, however, to do this without first understanding what Jesus Christ has done for you.

In Revelation 12:10 (NKJV) the devil is described as the accuser of the brethren. "Then I heard a loud voice saying in heaven, 'Now salvation, and strength, and the kingdom of our God, and the power of His Christ have come, for the accuser of our brethren, who accused them before our God day and night, has been cast down.'" It is the devil who accuses you, it is satan who has come to steal, kill, and destroy you, but it is Jesus who, through His death on the cross, has silenced the voice of satan forevermore!

In the last chapter we had a subtle glimpse into the book of Zachariah 3 (NKJV). I would like to unravel this beautiful picture even further, verse by verse. Verse one states, *"Then he showed me Joshua the high priest standing before the angel of the Lord, and satan standing at his right hand to oppose him.".* Imagine this. Joshua is before the Lord and the accuser is at his right hand ready to condemn, blame and chastise him! But the Lord says in verse two, *"The Lord rebuke you, satan! The Lord who has chosen Jerusalem rebukes you! Is not this a brand plucked out of the fire?"* The Lord is rebuking the accuser and silencing his charges, but in verse three something is brought to our attention. *"Now Joshua was clothed in filthy garments, and was standing before the Angel."* This third verse changes everything! If Joshua the high priest is clothed in that which is unclean, doesn't this give satan the right to accuse him? This is not so, for the Angel of the Lord, who is also known as Jesus Christ, rebukes the devil! Jesus strips the accuser of his power to accuse and silences the voice of condemnation! Joshua is filthy yet untouched by the enemy because he stands in the presence of God!

Few understand this incredible and life-changing truth about what Jesus has done for us. The Lord Jesus Christ has created for us a safe place to stand with our sin. When someone sins the first thing that the devil whispers is, *"hide."* The accuser tells you that you cannot enter the presence of the Lord with those filthy garments. He implores you to cover yourself in leaves so that the Lord will not see your sin. The voice of Satan is at odds with the voice of the Lord, for it is the voice of the Lord that calls to you in the midst of your darkness and says, *"come."* The voice of Jesus says, "come to me in your pain, filth, and sin and you will be safe here." In the presence of the Lord the devil loses his right to accuse you and Jesus silences his every attempt to speak a word against you.

There is one place where you are safe to stand with your sin and it is in the presence of God! Adam hid in the garden when he committed sin but the Lord called to him, "Adam where are you?" The Lord calls to us in our darkest moments. Jesus is able to handle our sin! He is the only one who can save us from it and the only one who can cleanse us of it! Every accusation dies at the feet of Christ Jesus!

Do not be ensnared by the lie that proclaims that you must be holy in order to receive the glory of the Lord. Embrace the truth that guarantees that it is *His* glory that will result in holiness within you! There are many who try to clean themselves before coming before the Lord, but if you were ever able to clean yourself then Jesus would not have come to die for your redemption. If you were ever able to clean yourself then the life and death of Jesus Christ would have been a waste. You see, when Joshua the high priest came into the presence of the Lord in his filthy garments, not only was the voice of satan silenced but something else incredible happened in verse four and five. *"Then he answered and spoke to those who stood before him, saying, 'Take away the filthy garments from him.' And to him He said, 'see I have removed your iniquity from you, and I will clothe you with rich robes.' And I said, 'Let them put a clean turban on his head.' So they put a clean turban on his head, and they put the clothes on him. And the angel of the Lord stood by."* When Joshua came into the presence of the Lord, it was Jesus who did the cleansing. It was Jesus who removed the dirty garments and replaced them with clean vestments! It is important that you understand that your job is to rise up and run to the presence of God, but the Lord does the rest! In Proverbs 24:16 we are told that it is, *"the righteous man"* who *"stumbles seven times."* The difference between the righteous man and the wicked man is that the wicked is *"destroyed by one disaster"* while the righteous man *"rises again!"* You see when the devil tells you to "stay down," or to hide yourself, when he comes to you with lies that speak of your desolation, all you must do is rise up and run to Jesus! Jesus is not ashamed of you. Rise up and run to your Redeemer, your Refiner, your Defender...you are safe in His arms!

There is something that you must know about your Savior. He responds to our betrayal with a covenant. On the very night that Jesus was betrayed His response was to break bread and say, *"This is my body, broken for you."* Every time we betray Him He comes with the covenant He has made *for us*, the covenant He has made *with us*, and He says, *"This is my body, broken for you, and this is my blood shed for the remission of your sins!"* Never let the enemy's voice hinder you from coming closer to Jesus Christ. It does not matter how messy or broken your life is... run to Jesus! When Joshua the high priest stood before the Lord and the enemy stood at his right hand, the enemy desired to gloat over Joshua's failure, but Jesus did something extraordinary. Jesus removed all the evidence of failure! Jesus replaced every proof of guilt with an exonerating and beautiful purity! When the enemy says, *"Look I see a sinner!"* Jesus asks *"Where?"* And Jesus looks at us as we stand in His presence and declares, *"I see no evidence of sin!"* He has made us righteous! Jesus took Joshua's filthy rags onto Himself and clothed Joshua with His own purity. He paid every penalty to free him from the voice of satan! Jesus has done this for each one of us! Satan has lost his right to accuse you. Remember, if ever the devil reminds you of your past, you can remind him of his future! *"Then I heard a loud voice saying in heaven, 'Now salvation, and strength, and the kingdom of our God, and the power of His Christ have come, for the accuser of our brethren, who accused them before God day and night, has been cast down" (Revelation 12:10 NKJV).* Satan has been cast down and silenced forevermore. Hallelujah!

**The Voice of the Law**

The second accuser is one who hides deep within the heart and often disguises itself in order to retain its power. The second accuser is the law. I would like you to understand something very important. The law was never created to serve you; in fact, the law was created to be against you. In Deuteronomy 31 Moses was at the end of his life. God told Moses that Joshua was going to lead Israel to the promised land. This chapter records the last time Moses is speaking to all the elders of Israel and he commands them, "Take this Book of the Law and put it by the side of the ark of the covenant of the Lord your God, that it may be there for a witness against you" (Deuteronomy 31:26 ESV).

Moses is the one who wrote the law and now we see that when he finished writing the law he requested that it would be near the arc of the covenant. The arc of the covenant was kept in the most holy place, a place where God dwelt; a place where the high priest could go only once a year; a place where one cannot enter without blood. The law was to be laid in the Holy of Holies next to the arc of the covenant, the very presence of God! I would like you to recall, however, that the law was placed in the most holy place to be a witness against you. The law was never created to be for you, but quite the opposite. The law was created to be against you. It is easy to believe that every accusation is from the devil, but satan cannot accuse you in the presence of the Lord. There is another accuser who meets you in the Holy of Holies, and his name is *the law*.

Moses is leaving the people with a *terrible* message! He states in Deuteronomy 31:27-28 (NKJV), *"For I know you are a rebellious people, a stiff neck people, I am yet alive with you, and you have been rebellious against the Lord how much more after my death? Gather to me all the elders of your tribe and your officers that I may speak these words in their hearing and call heaven and earth to witness against Israel."*

Moses is declaring that the law had become to them an accuser that would witness against them in the very presence of God. Secondly, Moses is saying that he has seen their rebellion and it would only grow worse after his death. Thirdly, Moses tells the people that heaven and earth will be turned against them! What misery do the Israelites find themselves in when heaven and earth have become their enemy! The law, which sits in the presence of God, has become their accuser! And rebellion, corruption, and evil, which are exceedingly worse than before, are promised to befall them. Moses even goes on to say in verse 29, *"You will do evil in the sight of the Lord to provoke him to anger through the work of your hands."* This is the news of the old covenant: accusation in the presence of the Lord, increasing failure and rebellion, cursed ground and sky, and worst of all, the anger of the Lord laid heavy on the shoulders and souls of the people. In the tabernacle of the Lord an accuser was waiting which is why the high priest would enter and fall dead if he had sinned. Deuteronomy 28 is filled with terrible curses for every mistake and shortcoming because the law was given to us as a witness against us.

Those last and terrible words of Moses became a song that was taught to many generations. The voice of accusation, despair and hopelessness became a song and what a painful song it was! How could you dance to a song that spoke of your unpreventable bondage? How could you hum to a tune that reminded you of your faults? My friend, I am here to tell you there is a new song; a beautiful song! This new song is a song you can dance to, a song you can hum, and sing, and scream at the top of your lungs! This is a song that Jesus wrote. Where the law accused, Jesus intercedes. Where the law condemned, the blood of Jesus defends! The death of Moses brought bondage and rebellion but the death of Jesus Christ brought freedom and righteousness! The death of Jesus Christ brought salvation and life!

Jesus even said it himself in John 5:45 (NKJV), "Do not think that I shall accuse you to the Father; there is *one* who accuses you—Moses, in whom you trust."

In John 8 there is a story of a woman who was caught in the act of adultery and those who brought her to Jesus said that *the law and Moses command that she be stoned*! Jesus responds with these words, "He who is without sin among you, let him throw a stone at her first" (John 8:7 NKJV). Jesus shielded the woman from condemnation and forgave her of all of her sin. Jesus does not accuse you - no! Jesus defends you. Jesus is your *great* protector.

When the woman who was caught in the act of adultery was brought to Jesus, Jesus banished her accusers and asked the woman, "*Where are your accusers? Has no one condemned you?*" The woman answered, "*No one, Lord.*" Jesus then said something that I pray will never leave your mind... "Neither do I condemn you." The only way that the accusations of the enemy, the accusations of the law, and the accusations of your own heart have any power is when you come into agreement with them! Do not agree with the voices of condemnation. Jesus does not condemn you. Jesus sees you as righteous, holy, and precious!

Our savior came to fulfill the law and rid it of all of its power. My friend, there is such joy in this new song! The old song says that you will be condemned and God's anger will be upon you. The new song says, "*Father, forgive them for they do not know what they do.*" The old song says that God will be angry with you, but the new song says that, "*It is finished*!" The anger, the pain, the misery, the hopelessness, the sin cycles, the accusations, the brokenness, and the condemnation - every chain brought by the law has been brought to an end! Jesus wrote for us a new song, His very blood speaks it from the ground. My friend, I implore you to ask yourself the question, *"Which song am I listening to?"* Even today both songs speak loudly. Where the old law remains there is a veil that is over the eyes, but the law has changed; there is a new priesthood and a new High Priest! Hebrews 7:12 (TPT) says, *"And furthermore, for God to send a new and different rank of priest, meant a new law would have to be instituted to even allow it!"* You are no more subject to the condemning voice who accuses you in God's presence! The new law comes from the life, truth, and way of Jesus Christ. In Romans 8:34 (NKJV) it is written, *"Who is he who condemns? It is Christ who died, and furthermore is also risen, who is even at the right hand of God, who also makes intercession for us."* Who can speak against us now? Jesus is the one who is interceding for us. The law and its condemnation was silenced the moment Jesus died on the cross. There is a new song!

**The Voice From Within**

The third voice is the one that comes from within. There is a self-condemning voice that will be silenced the closer you walk with the Lord, and to walk closely with the Lord you must accept His promises and truth. You have been conceived and born into a world of sin, and at times you may fall or stumble. There are moments when you will have an evil thought or feel broken beyond repair, but Jesus did not save you in order to demand perfection! Jesus has created a covenant of grace to secure true relationship as it was in the garden. No matter the mistakes you make or the places you fall short, you have become righteous in the sight of God because of the High Priest Jesus Christ.

Written on the forehead of your High Priest are the words *"holiness unto God."* Jesus Christ is your representative, so when God is looking at you He does not see your sin, He does not see your mistakes, He only sees holiness - the holiness of your High Priest! You are no longer judged based on your own thoughts and actions but on the thoughts and actions of the High Priest. Hallelujah!

Much of the damage that occurs within you does not come from what others tell you, but rather it comes from what you tell yourself! Proverbs 5:22 (TPT) states very clearly, *"Beware that your sins don't over take you and that the scars of your own conscience don't become the ropes that tie you up."*

The enemy has no power against you in the presence of God! When Jesus crushed his head, satan lost the right to tie you up. But if the enemy is not the one who ties you up, how then do you still find yourself in bondage? Proverbs says that it is *"the scars of your own conscience."* The voice of accusation inside of you comes from the experiences and feelings you have had, from the failures and mistakes you have made. It comes from the situations and circumstances that you face, and it grows with the lies you have heard and believed. This accusing voice is not external; it is internal. This voice prevents you from delighting in the Lord, it keeps you from finding rest in His arms, and often, this voice sends you running *from* His presence rather than running *to* His presence. The Lord, however, has made a way to walk in freedom from this voice of condemnation.

In 1 John 3 it tells us, *"If your heart condemns you, your God is bigger than your heart."* The truth of God is not in submission to our hearts, it is us who must submit our hearts to His truth! There are many problems that stem from listening too closely to one's heart. Offense, lies, and condemnation come from the heart and we are told in Jeremiah 17:9 (NKJV) that, *"The heart is deceitful above all things, and desperately wicked; who can know it?"* Oh, but *God is so much bigger than your heart*! God has given you the right to be free from condemnation and every accusing voice, including the one that comes from within!

There is away to be free of this voice, but it will be as difficult or as easy as you make it. To be free, all you must do is receive; you must receive the gift of righteousness. Righteousness is no longer a prize to be won; righteousness is a gift to be received! Your thoughts and feelings may urge you otherwise, but these things come from the heart and we know that God is so much greater, so much wiser and it is His truth that sets us free! Therefore, the only thing that is steady enough for you to build upon is the truth of God. Once you receive the gift of righteousness you will not only be able to rule over your own mind and life, but the scripture says that *"righteousness builds an entire nation" (Proverbs 14:34)*. The gift of righteousness is the hope of every nation and in turn, the hope of the world! The world cannot receive this blessed gift until the church does, so it is time. *Now* is the time for the church to be grounded in the greatest gift God gave to His children, His very own righteousness! Only in this reception can the condemning voice of your heart be silenced.

The lies that come from within have been stripped of their weight, for there is a greater voice!

## Sufficient Grace

Romans 8 (NKJV) says that *"the righteous requirement of the law might be fulfilled in us who do not walk according to the flesh but according to the Spirit"* which raises a necessary question. How does one walk according to the spirit? If you keep reading, the chapter states, *"For the law of the spirit of life in Christ Jesus has made me free from the law of sin and death."* The law that was set beside the arc of covenant produced in me sin and death but the law of the spirit of life, which is in Christ Jesus, has freed us all from such death. Just as there are two songs, there are also two laws. There is the old law of sin and death, which is the law that Moses wrote, but there is the new law of the spirit of life which is in Christ Jesus! Romans 8 continues by saying, *"what the law could not do in that it was weak, through the flesh God did by sending His own Son Jesus, in the likeness of sinful flesh on account of sin, He condemned sin in the flesh..."*

The law was placed in the presence of God to witness against you. It was never created to bring you the good news. It is incapable of doing so. But Jesus did! Jesus *is* the good news! One law was given and brought to us death, while the other brought to us everlasting life! The day the law was given to Moses three thousand died, but the day the Holy Spirit was released three thousand were filled and saved!

> One law was given and brought to us death, while the other brought to us everlasting life!

When Jesus died, His death was not just a historical event. The death of Jesus impacted our eternity forever so that our life no longer remains the same. The book of Ephesians explains to us, *"We who were destined to wrath and hell because of our sins, have been extended the mercy of God and that this mercy did not just restore us to the originality of Adam but we were made alive in the likeness of Jesus Christ the second Adam and we were made to sit together in heavenly places in Christ Jesus."* The law could never give us a resting place in the presence of God, but Jesus has. His grace has provided for us a seat to rest and a place to belong!

It would be a shame for one to believe that such a teaching is giving Christians the permission to sin without remorse, for this is a message of grace. It is written in Titus 2:12 (NIV) that His grace *"teaches us to say 'No' to ungodliness and worldly passions, and to live self-controlled, upright and godly lives in this present age."* Grace is the very thing that enables uprightness inside of us, so it is imperative that every person, church, and nation become acquainted with the new covenant of grace. Grace is not a license to sin; it is the path to freedom! Many of my students have begun to walk in freedom from sin not merely because of what I have taught them, but because they have chosen the song of Jesus and have plugged their ears to the song of condemnation! This grace, this freedom, is available to all, and it is satisfying and sustainable.

Hebrews 2:9 (NKJV) testifies to the beautiful grace of the Lord. *"That He, by the grace of God, might taste death for every man."* There was a time when this verse perplexed me greatly. I wondered what kind of grace would do this. The Lord, however, spoke to me and made it very clear. It was the grace of God that resurrected Jesus from the grave. It was His perfect grace that did not leave Jesus there, that let Him taste such darkness but never let it envelope Him! My friend, there is great pain in this world and many trials await you at every corner, but the grace of God will never leave you in the darkness, it will not abandon you there! When Paul cried out to the Lord three times asking to be healed, the Lord responded, *"My grace is sufficient"* (2 Corinthians 12:9 NIV). Do you understand what the Lord was saying? What pains you? What breaks you? What torments you? Here is my grace! What do you need? What do you desire? What are you seeking? Here is my grace, and it is enough.

We no longer go to a tabernacle since *we* ourselves have become *a tabernacle* for the Lord! The body is the outer court which is where priests would make a sacrifice, and so we must make our bodies as living sacrifices for the Lord. Now, the soul is the holy place and in the original holy place there was much light and new bread would be brought in every day. In this we discover that we are to feed our souls from the scriptures and be renewed by the power of His word. The spirit is the most holy place, the Holy of Holies! The problem with the human spirit is often we still set the law in our own hearts to be a witness against us, an accusing voice that is contradictory to the love of God. Have you ever wondered why you feel rejected from inside of yourself? The way of grace is calling to you! It is the way of freedom and Jesus is offering to you a new song; a beloved song. It's a song that says *"sin shall not have dominion over you, for you are not under law but under grace"* (Romans 6:14 NKJV). It's a song that promises that even when you taste death it will not overcome you, because grace will pull you out from the hands of darkness! It's a song that has granted you life and favor, a song of care that has preserved your soul! It's a song that has permanently cleansed your heart and renewed your spirit - a song that will never cast you out of the presence of God!

It is time to reprogram your heart. We were once *far off from Him, we were once His enemy,* but let this beautiful piece of scripture found in Colossians 1:22 take root in the soil of your heart. *"Now He has brought you back as his friends, He has done this through His death on the cross in His own human body. And as a result, He has brought you into the very presence of God, and you are holy and blameless as you stand before Him without a single fault."* This is the song that the Lord sings over you! Go boldly into His presence, for there is none to accuse you anymore! There is none to find fault in you anymore! You are decreed as *Holy unto God*! He does not accuse you; He speaks beautiful things over you. As it says in Romans 8:16 (TLB), *"his Holy Spirit speaks to us deep in our hearts and tells us that we really are God's children."* You are now His tabernacle. He abides in you and His voice is the only one that matters.

# Chapter 5

# Righteousness and Intimacy

Though grace is not given a particular definition in the Bible, you will see the beauty of God's grace on every page defined in a new way! Some have mistaken grace for forgiveness, but grace and forgiveness are two very different things. As an example, let's say that a man's only son was murdered. The father is now presented with a few options. The father could go to the law and legally have the offenders done away with. This would be justice. The father could find the offenders and take an eye for an eye, and a tooth for a tooth. He could repay their evil himself and this would be vengeance. The father also has the option to forgive the offenders and carry on with his life but still, this is not grace, this is a form of mercy. The grace option in this scenario does not end at simple forgiveness; it carries on far past that. Imagine that the father in this illustration finds his offenders and not only shows them mercy in full, but he gives the culprits his own name. With this new name those whom he could have punished are relieved of any charge that had been attached to their old names. The father does not stop there. He gives them the same authority that had belonged to his son, and blesses them in the same way that one blesses his own flesh and blood. This seems absurd! The grace option to human nature makes the least amount of sense. There is only one father I know who would choose such an option, and that is the Heavenly Father! You see, grace takes you beyond mercy; grace takes you into intimacy.

## The Parable of The Ten Virgins

In Matthew 24, Jesus is asked the question, *"what will be the sign of your coming?"* (Matthew 24:3 NASB). Jesus begins to teach the crowd about the end times and the signs of His return. Jesus explains how kingdoms will rise against kingdoms, that there will be wars and rumors of wars, earthquakes and natural disasters. Most of the signs that Jesus names are external.

One, however, is internal and it is the sign of *"love growing cold."* This context is especially important as we begin to study Matthew 25, the parable of the ten virgins, because this too is a response to the original question, *"What will be the signs of your return?"*

> *"The Kingdom of heaven can be illustrated by the story of ten righteous maids who took their lamps to meet the bridegroom. Five of them were foolish and five of them were wise. The five who were foolish took no oil for their lamps but the other five were wise enough to take along extra oil. When the bridegroom was delayed, they all laid down and slept and in the midnight hour they were roused by the shout. 'Look, the bridegroom is coming. Come out and welcome Him!' And the bridesmaids all got up and prepared their lamps. Then the five foolish ones asked the others, 'Please give me some of your oil, our lamps are going out' but the others replied 'We don't have enough for all of us, go to the shop and buy some for yourself.' While they were gone to buy the oil, the bridegroom came and those who were ready went in with him to the marriage feast and the door was locked. Later when the other five bridesmaids returned, they stood outside and called, 'Sir open the door for us' but He called back 'I do not know you.' So stay awake and be prepared because you do not know the day or the hour of His return".*

I had cultivated in my mind from a young age an idea that my salvation was very fragile. I once believed that one sinful act had the power to undo everything that Christ had done for me. Since my Sunday school days I was haunted by a lying voice that told me that I couldn't mess up or make a mistake and if I did, it would all fall apart! I didn't understand the extent of the grace of the Lord; I didn't understand His sacrifice. If the penalty for sin is death and Jesus died on my behalf, why then should I be living in fear of making a mistake?

The parable of the ten virgins has often sparked in people fear or guilt, but this is not what Jesus came to bring. The words of Jesus are meant to grant you life! The voice of the Lord authors faith, not condemnation. I would like to offer a new perspective on this parable, a perspective that does not involve guilt, fear or condemnation but rather increases faith in Jesus as our Bridegroom.

## The Oil

I have heard many messages and interpretations of this parable. Some say that the oil represents the Holy Spirit while others say that it represents intimacy with the Lord. I believe there is an even greater meaning in what the Lord is speaking through such a story.

If the oil is truly meant to represent the Holy Spirit, this alludes to the idea that the five wise maidens were unable to share the Holy Spirit with others. You must remember that the Holy Spirit does not run-out and when Jesus gifted to us His Spirit, He did not lose it. When Jesus gifted us the Holy Spirit He granted us access to a never-ending fountain of life! As we share this gift with others we do not lose it, instead we multiply it! There is another fault in this ideology - that it points to the fact that the ones who had the Holy Spirit believed it was something one could buy. The spirit of God, however, cannot be bought nor can it be sold! In Acts 8 Peter is approached by a magician named Simon. Simon had seen the signs and wonders of the Holy Spirit and desired to buy it. When Peter heard of Simon's intentions he spoke firmly saying, *"may your silver perish with you, because you thought you could obtain the gift of God with money" (Acts 8:20 ESV).* The Holy Spirit is not a thing you can buy or sell, trade or lose.The Holy Spirit is a free gift from the Father and none can take Him away from you.

The final fault in this way of thinking is that the wise maidens or those who were filled with the spirit had said to the foolish ones, *"go rather to the dealers and buy for yourselves"* (Matthew 25:9 ESV). We have established that the Holy Spirit cannot be lost when given, and that it cannot be bought or sold, so why would those who were filled with the spirit misguide the other five? The Spirit of God is the Spirit of truth and therefore the oil cannot represent the Holy Spirit.

Another belief regarding the oil in the parable is the idea that the oil is a symbol of intimacy with the Lord. It is true that you are unable to share someone else's intimacy. However, intimacy is, again, something that cannot be bought nor can it be sold. Intimacy is something you can only get from the one whom you desire to be intimate with.

Now, if the oil is neither the Holy Spirit nor is it intimacy, then what is it? I think that much can be uncovered by studying the Bridegroom in this story. We can be certain that the Bridegroom represents Jesus Christ and in this we know that those who are awaiting His arrival are a portrayal of the church. Jesus, in this parable is coming as a Bridegroom and so His return is for one purpose, the purpose of marriage, not judgment. The ten virgins are the church and represent believers such as you and I. You have become aware that in this parable half of the maidens are classified as foolish and half are classified as wise. It is important to understand why some are foolish and others are wise. Those who were foolish took their lamps without oil. It was not because they did not *have* oil that they were foolish; it was because they were *foolish* that they did not *take* oil! When Jesus speaks of the foolish man who builds on the sand and the wise man who builds on the rock and the difference between them, He explains that the wise man hears and obeys and the foolish man hears but does not change. When the Pharisees heard the parable about the sandy foundation they knew that Jesus was speaking about them. You must understand that wisdom and foolishness are not obtained by what you *have* but by what you choose as your foundation; what you build your life upon. The

> It was not because they did not have oil that they were foolish; it was because they were foolish that they did not take oil!

Pharisees chose religion and empty routines as their bedrock and the Lord labeled them as foolish and hypocritical! As you read and study the word of God you will discover that there is always a counterfeit path that may seem righteous but leads away from the Lord.

In the parable of the ten virgins we can clearly identify the counterfeit path and establish what the true foundation is. The Bridegroom was never coming for oil; the Bridegroom was coming for a bride. The Bridegroom did not need a lamp; the Bridegroom needed a bride! It is astonishing how your lens and focus can change everything. The object of the parable shifts drastically when you remove the oil from the center.

## Comparison and Self-Focus

I would like to reevaluate this parable with this new perspective. All the maidens were desperate to meet the Bridegroom, they all loved Him dearly. The ten maidens wore their bridal attire, they awoke at the midnight hour, they brought with them their burning lanterns and they all fell asleep, the wise and the foolish alike. They all heard the voice of the coming Bridegroom, they all awoke together and all began to trim their lamps. Up until this point there is no problem at all. Finally the trouble is discovered and five maidens see that their lamps are flickering, and they realize at this moment that they are out of oil! Now, when these girls left their homes they were not conscious of the supply of their oil. These five maidens were not conscious of their lack of oil as they went on their way, nor were they conscious of this when they slept. It was only when the five maidens awoke and began to rekindle their lamps that they began to see that their lamps were flickering. I would like you to notice something very interesting. Though the lamps of the five foolish maidens were not as bright as the others, their lamps were never put out; they were still burning.

The first thing that goes wrong in this moment is that the maidens whose lamps where dim began to focus on their oil, they began to focus on their lamps, and ultimately on themselves. They began to take their eyes off of the coming Bridegroom and place them instead on their own failures and faults. Something treacherous began to overtake the five foolish maidens - comparison! All ten brides awaited their Groom in unity until five looked at the others, then back at themselves, and their perspective shifted from the coming Groom to fear of failure! Questions and doubts began to flood the hearts of the foolish maidens and they saw nothing but themselves. This is a mirror of what happened at the fall of creation.

When Adam and his wife ate of the fruit and committed the first sin, the very next thing to happen was they saw themselves naked. Since the beginning of the world sin has played the same tricks and swindled in the same manner. Sin attempts to steal our gaze so that all we see is our own brokenness and in turn, it blots out the grace and beauty of the Lord. A sin focused person is susceptible to a religious spirit and a religious spirit is a spirit of lies, convincing us that we must qualify for the love of God when in reality, Jesus has already qualified us!

Comparison is a fleshly tendency and it leads to a desire to recreate something that isn't our own. Comparison is a path to hypocrisy and breeds copies. It slaughters anything that is unique and discourages all potential for what is great and what is new! When the five foolish virgins saw that the others had brighter lamps, they began to desire what wasn't theirs, asking for oil that didn't belong to them. The eyes of the five foolish girls coveted the others and they pleaded, *"Give us some of your oil!"* The foolish ones believed that the other maidens were what the Bridegroom was expecting and they became ashamed of themselves. *"Give us some of your oil, so that we can be like you!"* Often when we begin to fall into comparison it is easy to elevate man to the place of God and expect a man to lead us. You must understand that to seek answers from man in place of God is pain, confusion and death! Jesus warns us of several traps in the last days… beware of the distracting and destroying spirit of comparison, do not let men become your source, do not disconnect from the vine, don't take your gaze off of your first love!

## The Character of the Bridegroom

When the brides turned their eyes from the Groom, there was another terrible thing that happened… they forgot His character.

The character of the Bridegroom is marvelous. *"A bruised reed He will not break, and a smoldering wick He will not snuff out"* (Isaiah 42:2 ESV). The Groom, in whom we await, is the one who breathes life into parts of us that are flickering. Jesus has regard for the pieces of ourselves that we deem as weak or unfit. In *the parable of the sower* Jesus speaks about the *good* soil, and we can rest assured that what Jesus calls good is truly good! When speaking about the good soil Jesus explains that it will bear thirty fold, sixty fold, and one hundred fold. Jesus does not say that the foolish and evil will bear thirty fold and the wise and righteous will bear one hundred fold… no! Jesus calls the soil *good* and in doing so, He is calling the thirty percent good, the sixty percent good and the one hundred percent good as well! This is the Lord's character. He is the one who does not despise small beginnings and He does not reject those with the smallest of flames. Psalms 138:6 (NKJV) states, *"Though the Lord is on high, Yet He regards the lowly."* This is the character of the Groom whom we await!

The foolish maidens were striving to become acceptable to the Groom by their own works, but from Ephesians 2:8-9 (NIV) we know, *"It is by grace you have been saved, through faith—and this is not from ourselves, it is the gift of God— not by works, so that no one can boast."* The foolish girls were not receiving by faith; they were attempting to gain through vain works. The five foolish virgins had fallen into the same trap as the church of Galatians when Paul wrote to them, *"Who has bewitched you?"* (Galatians 3:1 ESV). Paul questions, *"Having begun by the Spirit, are you now being perfected by the flesh?"* (Galatians

> There is only one hope and it is not in the brightness of your lamp, but in the brightness of the One and only light of the world!

3:3 ESV). The Lord is speaking to the brides who are holding flickering lanterns and He is asking them, *"Who has bewitched you? Who has deceived you? Who has told you that you were naked?"* The devil desires to instill fear in your heart, he longs for you to distrust the character of your Groom and the perfect grace of your savior. In Jeremiah 17:5 (NLT) it is written, *"Cursed are those who put their trust in mere humans, who rely on human strength and turn their hearts away from the Lord."* The foolish virgins had misplaced their trust; they had misplaced their hope! David writes in Psalms 62:5 (ESV), *"For God alone, O my soul, wait in silence, for my hope is from him."* There is only one hope and it is not in the brightness of your lamp, but in the brightness of the One and only light of the world! Every fear and doubt arises from a lack of knowledge of the character of the Lord for his *"promises are backed by the honor of (his) name"* (Psalms 138:2 NLT).

In Isaiah we hear many descriptions of the character of God. Isaiah 26:3 (NIV), *"You will keep in perfect peace those whose minds are steadfast, because they trust in you."* Isaiah 64:4 (NIV), *"Since ancient times no one has heard, no ear has perceived, no eye has seen any God besides you, who acts on behalf of those who wait for him."* All we do is wait, and He acts on our behalf! We must learn the character of our bridegroom or else we may fall into deceitful traps that the enemy sets for us. In Isaiah 1:3 (NIV) it is said, *"The ox knows its master, the donkey its owner's manger, but Israel does not know, my people do not understand."* It is time for the Bride to learn the character of her Bridegroom!

The parable of the ten virgins is setting the tone for the New Covenant of Grace! This parable is not about the oil and it is not about the flame, it is about a gracious Groom coming for His bride! The foolish maids began to work in the flesh, trying to manufacture a confidence and righteousness outside of the gift that the Lord has offered. In Romans 10:3 (NIV) we read, *"Since they did not know the righteousness of God and sought to establish their own, they did not submit to God's righteousness."* There is a counterfeit oil that the foolish search for in the marketplaces of the world, but the world and its wicked ways are perishing! You cannot find or manufacture your own righteousness, it comes from one man. *"For if, by the trespass of the one man, death reigned through that one man, how much more will those who receive God's abundant provision of grace and of the gift of righteousness reign in life through the one man"* (Romans 5:17 NIV). The foolish maids were foolish because they did not make the wise choice of understanding that the gift of righteousness is a free gift. They wanted to pay for what is free, but in John 1:16 we are told that, *"From the fullness of His grace, we have received one blessing after another."* We receive from one place and that is the fullness of His grace!

> The foolish maids were foolish because they did not make the wise choice of understanding that the gift of righteousness is a free gift.

When the maids discovered their light was flickering they searched for aid everywhere except in the one who was full of grace and ready to pour out endless blessings. It was because of this that the door was shut. The Lord will never open the door for what you do on your own in order to earn His free gifts. It is an insult to the sacrifice of Jesus Christ to try and justify ourselves when He has offered us freedom through covenant with Him! 2 Corinthians 3:4-6 (ESV) tells us,

> *"Such is the confidence that we have through Christ toward God. Not that we are sufficient in ourselves to claim anything as coming from us, but our sufficiency is from God, who has made us sufficient to be ministers of a new covenant, not of the letter but of the Spirit. For the letter kills, but the Spirit gives life."*

So many have heard the parable of the ten virgins and have taken it as an instruction to fear and strive, but it is quite the opposite! When the Groom arrived, He did not judge the wise for falling asleep, He did not condemn them for misdirecting the foolish, the Groom simply took them in because His grace has covered every fault and every mistake. He gave power only to the ones who believed in Him and He did not give power to the ones who did not believe. Everything in the Word points to the reliability of the grace of the Lord. His righteousness is our qualification! We are children of the Lord and children do not have to earn the love of a good father, they only have to receive it.

There is one last piece of scripture I would like to bring to your mind. These passages have terrified many but they can only instill fear in those who do not truly know the character of their Groom. Hebrews 10:26-29 (ESV) tells us,

> *"If we go on sinning deliberately after receiving the knowledge of the truth, there no longer remains a sacrifice for sins, but a fearful expectation of judgment, and a fury of fire that will consume the adversaries. Anyone who has set aside the law of Moses dies without mercy on the evidence of two or three witnesses. How much worse punishment, do you think, will be deserved by the one who has trampled underfoot the Son of God, and has profaned the blood of the covenant by which he was sanctified, and has outraged the Spirit of grace?"*

When we read these passages without any context there is a fear that arises. You even might begin to recount all of your many mistakes and feel as though you have something to make up for. This passage, if it is set beside the parable of the ten virgins, seems as though a life with God is too far out of reach! When you are studying the Bible, however, the context is cardinal and so often overlooked.

You cannot begin to try and understand Hebrews 10 if you have not first begun to understand the previous nine chapters! Throughout the whole book of Hebrews we are becoming aware of the superiority of Jesus Christ and the inferiority of the law. Hebrews 1-9 explains to us that Jesus is far greater than any and all of the Old Testament prophets. We are being taught in chapter 10 that the sacrifice of Jesus Christ reigns unrivaled. No blood, no flesh, no sacrifice of any animal compares to the blood and flesh and sacrifice of Jesus the Christ. Jesus is superior over all the angels and the archangels, Jesus is superior over the tabernacle of Moses, and Jesus is superior over all the high priests, for He is the High Priest after the order of Melchizedek, and He is the only way! The book of Hebrews explains how in the days of old God would speak through prophets, but we are now in the time where God speaks to us through the mouth of His own son! If you understand that Hebrews 10 is merely confirming these truths, then this once bitter and painful passage becomes a seal on that which God has already established within your heart. The writer of Hebrews from chapter one has been preparing you for the grave message in chapter ten. He is saying that there is no other way but Jesus. The old ways are no more. The old ways lead to destruction and were never meant to fulfill you, but rather point you to the true way - Jesus! This passage in Hebrews 10 is explaining to us that Jesus is the only hope, He is the living hope, and if we reject Him then we are without hope. If we turn back to our works and religious acts in an attempt to justify ourselves, we have chosen an inferior law, which is the law of sin and death! If one were to reject the greatest and final sacrifice that takes away the sin of the world, then there would be no sacrifice left for that person.

The message in Hebrews 10:26-29 is quite simple. If you nullify the sacrifice of the cross by placing your hope and confidence in your works, in your ways, and in yourself then you will perish. You will deprive the cross of its power. The five foolish maidens looked to their oil to determine their standing with the Groom, but it was not the oil that the Groom was coming for... He was coming back for the maidens themselves. Hebrews 10 is telling us that everything leading up to Jesus was simply preparing *for* Him. It is telling us to withdraw our trust from our own works and to put our trust in Jesus who reigns above all! We trample the spirit of Grace and the sacrifice of Jesus when we choose to put our faith in our own ways; but when we choose to rely on Jesus and His ways, that is where true life is born.

I pray that you will begin to see yourself differently over the course of this book and that you will no longer associate yourself with failure and sin but that you would begin to see yourself the way the Father sees you. Where you see a maiden who lacks oil, the Lord sees a beautiful bride who He has been awaiting! You must turn your gaze from what those around you are doing, how bright their lamps are burning, and how much oil they possess, and you must fix your eyes on the Bridegroom! The Bridegroom is coming back for *you*, not what you have to offer, not a collection of achievements, not your many efforts. Jesus is coming back for you, and you are very precious to Him. It is time to start seeing yourself through the eyes of your Father.

> Where you see a maiden who lacks oil, the Lord sees a beautiful bride who He has been awaiting!

Chapter 6

# Righteousness and Oneness with God

A couple of years ago the Lord spoke to me about the condition of the church that I was pastoring. Our people were still suffering even after being born again. They were still wrestling with sin cycles and a lack of identity. I began to realize that much of the congregation was stuck in the elementary teachings of the Word of God. If they continued to be caught up in the issues of religion and the law, I knew this would only lead them into further bondage. As I sought the Lord, He said to me, *"Son, teach them my Word so that their lives will be rooted and grounded in righteousness, that they would receive the gift of righteousness and live from my finished works, and not from their works."*

We are often taught that we will reap what we sow, but Jesus stood in the gap for us and created a new way and a New Covenant. We now reap from what He has sown! Jesus Himself spoke the words, *"seek first the kingdom of God and His righteousness, and all these things shall be added to you"* (Matthew 6:33 NKJV). There is no facet of our life on Earth which is outside the domain of righteousness and there is no part of us that is not connected to our creator and His great victory.

In 1 Peter 1:3 (ESV) it is written, *"Blessed be the God and Father of our Lord Jesus Christ! According to his great mercy, he has caused us to be born again to a living hope through the resurrection of Jesus Christ from the dead."* This is such an extraordinary picture of what Jesus has done for us. You and I are born again, not through Jesus' suffering, death, and burial, but rather you and I are born again through His resurrection! In this we see and know something beautiful; our born again experience begins in victory.

When you are born again you are born into victory - victory over sin, over hell, over satan, and over death! You are not born only *for* victory, but you are born *from* victory! Now, there is something very important that I pray you will begin to understand. In the same way that you are not *for* victory but you are *from* victory, so it is that you are not just *for* heaven but you are *from* heaven!

## The Heavenly Man

Our minds naturally associate new words and phrases with something familiar and relatable. It is easy to default to what we know when at times, it is what we do not yet know that we must fight to find. It is often what is not yet established that must be built up in order to transform us. The title "The Heavenly Man" could easily be associated with Jesus Christ, but in this chapter I invite you to begin to associate yourself with this title in a new way!

The famous verse, John 3:16 (NKJV), tells us *"For God so loved the world that He gave His only begotten Son, that whoever believes in Him should not perish but have everlasting life."* Jesus was not given to us so that we would be granted a heavenly experience once we die. Jesus was given to us in order to grant us eternal life in its fullness the moment that we believe in Him! The instant you choose Jesus as your savior, you are permitted access to eternity. Your eternity is not based on you, or what you have accomplished, or what you have to offer; your eternity is based on the victory of your savior.

In 1 Corinthians 15 Paul is writing to the church in Corinth. The church of Corinth is a diverse crowd of Jews and Gentiles and Paul begins his teaching with the Gospel. I believe this is very important because Paul is assuring the church that this is no new teaching or ideology, it is rather the same Gospel being made manifest within each of us! In verse 45 (NIV) we are told, *"'The first man Adam became a living being'; the last Adam, a life-giving spirit."* The first man Adam is the Adam who was put in the garden, the first man ever created. Our God breathed life into the nostrils of this man and from this breath a living being was created. The second Adam, Jesus Christ, did not only become a living being but when God breathed into this man He became a life-giving spirit! The first Adam was alive but could not *give* life. He was a recipient of life but he could not extend it. The second Adam could resurrect the dead. He was a giver of life. The second Adam when introduced to death brings life; when met by darkness brings light. Anything broken before Him will be made new again. Verse 46 (ESV) tells us, *"But it is not the spiritual that is first, but the natural and then the spiritual."* Now, there is something that you must begin to understand before we continue further. Adam was not spiritual. The very first Adam was actually a natural man.. Many preach that Jesus died in order to make us in the likeness of Adam before the fall of creation, but this is false. Jesus did not die to make us in the likeness of Adam but in the likeness of Himself, the second Adam! Jesus does not only make us new, He makes us better than we were before! In the very next verse it says that, *"The first man was of the earth, made of dust; the second Man is the Lord from heaven"* (1 Corinthians 15:47 NKJV). The first man is *from* dust and will return *to* dust, but the second man is not from the ground. He, in fact, is not a product of earth at all. The second Adam is *from* heaven and this is why the word concerning Him says, *"You will not allow your Holy One to see decay"* (Psalms 16:10 AMP). After Jesus was crucified on the cross he did not stay in the grave, He arose and conquered death. It is this man, the man from heaven, the man who overcame the grave, the man who brings life into dead places… it is Him whom we are being made in the likeness of!

David spoke these words, *"In sin, I was conceived in my Mother's womb"* (Psalms 51:5). Truly, these words are accurate for all of us. We are all born into a world of sin; we are all born carrying the design of the first Adam. If, however, we look at 1 Corinthians 15 again, there is something great to be discovered in verse 49 (NKJV). *"And as we have borne the image of the man of dust, we shall also bear the*

> There was a time in which we bore the image of the man of dust, but it is now time to bear the image of the heavenly man!

*image of the heavenly man."* We are born into the natural, but we are reborn into the supernatural! There was a time in which we bore the image of the man of dust, but it is now time to bear the image of the heavenly man! When you are born again, you are no longer under the identity of the man of dust but you now share the image of the man of heaven.

In John 8:23 (NIV) Jesus says, *"You are from below; I am from above. You are of this world; I am not of this world."* When Jesus spoke these words He was speaking to the Jewish leaders. Jesus was not declaring this over His believing disciples; rather, this was a message for those who were still bound by the law. Jesus was born *on* the earth, but He knew His identity was not *from* the earth. Jesus says this Himself in John 3: *"If you do not believe me when I tell you about things that happen here on earth, how can you possibly believe when I tell you what is going on in heaven? For only I the son of man have come to earth and will return to heaven again."* Jesus knew His identity and now it is time for us to know ours.

Jesus spoke of how He was going away to prepare a place for us. He told the disciples that they *know the way* and that they must believe! When we hear such verses it is easy to conclude that Jesus is *from* heaven and we are only *for* heaven. There is a marvelous thing, however, that is found in John 17. In this chapter there is a conversation that is recorded. This conversation is not between Jesus and the Jewish leaders, nor is it between Jesus and the disciples. In John 17:14 (NLT) Jesus is speaking to the Father. He says, *"I have given them your word. And the world hates them because they do not belong to the world."* Jesus is saying that He has given them the Father's *word*, but what is the word?

John 1 tells us that in the beginning was the word, *"and the Word became flesh and dwelt among us, and we beheld His glory, the glory as of the only begotten of the Father"* (John 1:14 NKJV). Jesus is saying through this verse that He has given Himself to the disciples and they no longer belong to this earth! Now, belonging and destination are two very different things.

As a born again child of the Lord you must understand that your destination is not heaven, you already belong *to* heaven. A very dire problem occurs when you begin to make heaven your destination. If you make your destination heaven you will then try not to miss heaven; you will then try not to lose heaven. If, however, you discover that you already belong *to* heaven the characteristics of heaven will naturally flow through you. You see, whatever you belong to you will represent. Jesus is saying to the Father, *"Father, I have given them your word; I have given them myself and they no longer belong to this earth!"* If we read further in John 17 Jesus continues, *"I'm not asking you to take them out of the world, but to keep them safe from the evil one. They do not belong to this world any more than I do"* (John 17:15-16 NLT). Jesus in saying this is giving them a new identity; an identity that mirrors His own and an identity that names them citizens of heaven! Let me explain when Holy Spirit came upon virgin Marry and she conceived and Jesus was born. The same Holy Spirit latter in Acts chapter 2, came upon 120 people at upper room and The Church was born. You see our birth process is same like Jesus therefore we also are from heaven.

Those who belong to heaven must learn to live heavenly lives, and we learn this from the Father. A child speaks the same language as his father not in order to become his father's son but because he *is* his father's son. In the same way, we are to live heavenly lives not because we desire to belong to heaven, but because we *do* belong to heaven! Jesus continues and asks the Father to, *"Make them holy by your truth; teach them your word, which is truth. Just as you sent me into the world, I am sending them into the world"* (John 17:17-18 NLT). When we are reborn into God's kingdom we become citizens of heaven. We become children of the Lord and our Father begins to teach us His ways, the ways of the place in which we have been born into - heaven! Jesus is asking the Father to sanctify the believers. Jesus knew that if the Father would train them, teach them, and guide them as they walked through the world they would know their true identity. Jesus knew that the true identity of the disciples was not anything that they could find on earth for they were citizens of heaven and alien to this world!

It is easy to fall into a dangerous trap that tells us that we must live holy in order to be accepted by the Lord, but Jesus did not bring us this message. This mindset is still under that of the Old Testament. In the days of old they would sanctify themselves for three days before the Lord could meet them in their camp. The old law tells us to purify ourselves to meet God but the new law tells us to come in our filthy rags and let the Lord be the one to purify us. When the father saw from a distance his prodigal son coming home, the rags that his son wore did not disappoint him. The father did not first demand that his son change his clothes, shower, and apply expensive perfumes. The father saw his son, ran to him and embraced him, and then, and only then did he have his son cleaned and adorned with a new robe, a ring and sandals. The new covenant is, "acceptance *first* and achievement *next.*" The heavenly Father accepts you because you belong to Him. Your Father accepts you first and then He begins to teach you how to live like Him.

> The old law tells us to purify ourselves to meet God but the new law tells us to come in our filthy rags and let the Lord be the one to purify us.

In John 17:19 (NLT) Jesus tells the Father something magnificent! *"I give myself as a holy sacrifice for them so they can be made holy by your truth."* Jesus committed Himself fully into the hands of His Father so that we could be qualified and so that we could run into the Father's arms! Jesus did not only do this for His disciples, but He did this for everyone who believes. He states this Himself in the next verse, *"I am praying not only for these disciples but also for all who will ever believe in me."* In one sentence Jesus expands this extraordinary invitation to the whole world;to anyone who believes! You can now place yourself into the equation. Jesus is praying for you. Jesus is interceding for you. Jesus is speaking to the Father about *you*!

You are not from this earth, you are born again under a new name. You are wiped clean and given brand new software. Jesus Christ has labeled you as His own and the Father will guide and keep you as you walk through this estranged world. When Jesus gave Himself entirely to the Father He made a way for your complete acceptance and rebirth!

## One Spirit

Jesus continues to speak to the Father on our behalf and there is something very specific that He asks for. *"My prayer for all of them is that they will be one, just as you and I are one. Father as You are in me and I in you, so they will be in us and the world will believe you sent me."* When the revelation of the truth of God comes over you you become one with Him, as it is written in 1 Corinthians 6:17, *"He who fellowships with the Lord becomes one spirit with Him."* We have established throughout this book that you are made up of three parts: a spirit, a soul(mind), and a body. 1 Thessalonians 5:23 (ESV) tells us, *"Now may the God of peace Himself sanctify you completely, and may your whole spirit and soul and body be kept blameless at the coming of our Lord Jesus Christ."* This verse defines us in three ways, and I would like to dive deeper into the salvation of our spirit, soul, and body.

When we are born again the first thing to be transformed is our spirits. The moment that Jesus saved you, your spirit became one with God! This is why the Bible describes those who are in Christ as *"a new creation."* Christ has put His spirit within us and we have become one spirit with Him. One candle is often used to spread light to many other candles. The fire itself is not changed when it is passed from one candle to the next, for it is the same fire. So it is with the spirit of God. The spirit within you is the spirit of God. When you were reborn, your spirit was merged and joined together with the very spirit of God and this fire spread! The fire of God's spirit cannot be diluted, it cannot be changed, and in the moment you were born again your spirit is fully saved by becoming one with God's spirit.

When your spirit is born again your mind may cling to its old habits and think in its old ways. Your soul and mind after being reborn must be transformed as it is said in Romans 12:2 (NLT), *"Don't copy the behavior and customs of this world, but let God transform you into a new person by changing the way you think. Then you will learn to know God's will for you, which is good and pleasing and perfect."* The renewal of our minds involves us taking action, but not with our own strength! God's spirit is within you and through the strength of *His* spirit and the power of His word, you acquire the ability to train your mind to function in the way that God intended it to function. Through the revelation of Christ and the alignment of your mind with His mind, you will begin to see the world differently. You will begin to think and see like Jesus does. The Bible commands us to *"walk in the Spirit" (Galatians 5:16)* in order to refrain from falling into the lust of the flesh. In order to train your mind, you must stop living from your soul and instead begin living from your spirit, for it has become one with God's Spirit.

If a wealthy man were to adopt a poor boy off the streets, the boy would come under a new roof and a new name. If this boy, however, does not change his way of thinking then he will continue to live in fear of starvation; in fear of lack. The boy may be presented with a bountiful feast and yet he would still hide handfuls of food inside of his pockets believing that it will never come again. We have a good and patient Heavenly Father when we are experiencing difficulty while changing our mindset. When we still hide food in our pockets and fall into old habits, our Heavenly Father has a beautiful response. The response of our Father toward our brokenness and failures is simply to teach us!

This is why when Jesus was interceding for us to the Father in John 17:17 (NLT) he said, *"Make them holy by your truth; teach them your word, which is truth."* Do you see the wonderful order of the grace of God? The Lord's order is acceptance first, and then next is the cleaning; the teaching and then the achievement. In the analogy of the adopted son who was brought in from the streets, he was first adopted before he was taught to renew his mind and change his old habits. Your spirit is already saved; you are already accepted. It is simply time to change your mindset. Your mind begins to change through your choice to no longer live by your mind but by your spirit and to let the Lord and His spirit guide and teach you!

The final thing to be renewed is our physical body. It is true that we can receive healing after being saved but when I speak of the word renewal I am referring to what 2 Corinthians 5:4 (NLT) is saying, *"While we live in these earthly bodies, we groan and sigh, but it's not that we want to die and get rid of these bodies that clothe us. Rather, we want to put on our new bodies so that these dying bodies will be swallowed up by life."* Paul is explaining that even though now we dwell in bodies that are subjected to the darkness of this world, this will not always be the case. Our bodies are those that are prone to pain and sickness, age and death, groaning and sighing, but a day is coming when we will cast them off and receive our new bodies. The Bible tells us that when Jesus returns, our bodies will be transformed into glorious bodies, new and perfect.

My spirit within me has been saved and united with God's spirit the moment I was born again. My mind is coming into alignment with my newborn spirit by the power of Christ and His word and life that is in me. The very body in which I live will soon be transformed into God's beautiful design, untouched by darkness and fully eternal. Praise be to God forever!

## Children of God

There are many who still struggle with the concept of acceptance. It is easy to continue to strive for God's love and grace when in fact, He has given it freely. Those who do not understand how the Lord sees them are prone to fall into the many traps of the enemy. 1 John 3:1-3 (NKJV) states,

> *"Behold what manner of love the Father has bestowed on us, that we should be called children of God! Therefore the world does not know us, because it did*

> *not know Him. Beloved, now we are children of God; and it has not yet been revealed what we shall be, but we know that when He is revealed we shall be like Him, for we shall see Him as He is. And everyone who has this hope in Him purifies himself, just as He is pure."*

The first thing that we must note about these wondrous verses is that John is establishing something very urgent through them. We are children of God, very *dear* children who are loved inexplicably by their Father! We are informed through these verses that, *"the world does not know us because it did not know Him!"* So in this, we are told specifically how the world sees us and specifically how God sees us. The world does not know Him and therefore they do not know those who belong *to* Him. The world desired to stone Jesus for His claims to be the Son of God. They were met by something they could not fully comprehend and so they labeled it as wrong. The Father does not see us as the world does, but rather sees us as His very own, dearly loved children!

It is very important to evaluate the view you have of yourself. Do you see yourself as a dearly loved child of God or do you see yourself as someone who is unfit and unlovable? If you are not seeing yourself in the way that God sees you then you are seeing yourself in the way that the world sees you and this is very dangerous!

In verse three John says that, *"Everyone who has this hope in Him purifies himself, just as He is pure."* This perfect hope that the Lord grants you is not only sustaining you through hardships and difficulties but it is also purifying you! You see, it is not fear that purifies you but hope; nor is it judgment that makes you holy, but rather acceptance from the Father! Jesus had said to the Father in John 17:19, *"I give myself holy to you so that they will be holy."* In 1 Thessalonians 5:23 (ESV) it reiterates this point when it says, *"Now may the God of peace himself sanctify you completely, and may your whole spirit and soul and body be kept blameless at the coming of our Lord*

*Jesus Christ."* It is not our own hands that purify us but it is God Himself who purifies us because we belong to Him! Begin to let your eyes transform into *His* eyes and see yourself the way your Heavenly Father sees you.

1 Thessalonians 5:5 (ESV) says, *"For at one time you were darkness, but now you are light in the Lord. Walk as children of light."* Through this verse Paul is not claiming that you were once *in* the darkness, but rather he is stating that you once *were* the darkness. Again, Paul is not professing that you are now *in* the light, Paul is assuring you that you have now become *the* light! If you pay close attention to the phrasing in this verse you will recognize something astounding. We are not being commanded to walk as children of light so that we can become light, but rather the opposite! We are being informed through this verse that since we *are* light we are made able to walk as children of light.

A saying that has been proven to be true states that *"hurt people hurt people."* What I have also found to be true is that healthy people refrain from inflicting pain on others. When someone is wounded and wrestling with rejection it is that person who is prone to the attacks and traps of the enemy. When you understand what Jesus has done for you and what He says about you, and truly, truly how He sees you, sin will then have no more ammunition to oppose you with!

In the same letter in which Paul names those of this church *"children of light,"* he also addresses many of their imperfections. This observation speaks deeply. The church in which Paul is addressing is struggling and failing in certain places but this does not sever their sonship. Paul continues to name them *"children of light"* because salvation and adoption is not perfection. The order of the Kingdom of God is *acceptance first* and everything else follows after.

The concept of acceptance is a major building block in our foundation and it cannot be skipped or else the fortress will come crumbling down! It is important that you fully embrace and walk in the identity that the Lord has fashioned specifically for you.

Romans 8:29-31 (NLT) reveals an extravagant and freeing truth about you and I.

> *"For God knew His people in advance, and He chose them to become like His Son, so that His Son would be the firstborn among many brothers and sisters. And having chosen them, He called them to come to Him. And having called them, He gave them right standing with Himself. And having given them right standing, He gave them His glory."*

The first thing I would like to address is the first three words, *"For God knew."* The prophet Jeremiah tells us that before he was even formed in his mother's womb the Lord knew him and had already called him into his identity. God knows, and He knew it all before it even happened. God knew that you would be born into sin. He knew the mistakes that you were going to make. He knew the sin and failure that you were going to fall into. The Lord's knowledge of your faults did not stop Him from choosing you. The Lord saw you just as you are and still chose to adopt you; He still chose to draw you near to Him and make you like Him!

Our savior did not come to this earth to judge, but to save and to bestow on us the gift of righteousness! It is so beautiful to know this one thing: God knew you. He knew that you were a sinner and yet He did not reject you. The Lord did not condemn you but instead made a way for you to come close to Him and to become like Him! Hallelujah!

The next segment of this verse unveils something truly incredible. *"He chose them to become like His Son, so that His Son would be the firstborn among many brothers and sisters."* Now there is a famous passage from the book of John that tells us that God gave His *only begotten son (John 3:16).* My friend, when Jesus died on the cross He died as the only begotten Son of God. The very moment that Jesus rose up from the grave, however, He became the first born of many! Jesus Christ is now the first born of everyone who believes. God no longer has one son but each of us have been born again as sons and daughters of the Heavenly Father! Of course our God never stops at the quota but He goes far beyond it. The next section of this verse states, *"And having chosen them, He called them to come to Him."* You are chosen and called to be close to the Lord! *"And having called them, He gave them right standing with Himself."* You have been gifted righteousness through the victory of Christ Jesus! *"And having given them right standing, He gave them His glory."* You are adorned in the glory of God, clean and spotless before Him. This is your inheritance! You were never destined to fight for your sonship because it is who you are; you are a child of God. You were never meant to strive to be close to your Father because He Himself is pulling you into His arms. You were never supposed to follow rules to become righteous, you have been declared righteous by your savior. The glory of God has been given to you because you are His heir and His dearly loved child; this is how the Lord sees you!

There are many places in each of our lives that must grow and continue to be transformed and there are aspects of each of us that are very messy and imperfect. You must understand that no mistake that you make or failure you succumb to could ever change the place in which you stand with God. The Lord knows every part of you that you are ashamed of and He is not ashamed of you. We are told in Hebrews 2:11 (NLT), *"So now Jesus and the ones He makes holy have the same Father. That is why Jesus is not ashamed to call them His brothers and sisters."* There is a significant difference between how the world sees you and how the Lord sees you. *"If you were of the world, the world would love you as its own; but because you are not of the world but I chose you out of the world, therefore the world hates you."* You are

> You now bear the image of the Man in the garden of gethsemane who crushed the power of sin forever!

estranged to this world. You are not of it and you are not from it. You are no longer bearing the identity of the man in the Garden of Eden who brought sin into this world. You now bear the image of the Man in the garden of gethsemane who crushed the power of sin forever! It is time for you to understand your true identity. There is no more room for striving to get to heaven and fearing the wrath of the Father. You are not *for* heaven, but you are *from* heaven and you are no longer an orphan, but you have been grafted into the family of Christ. You are the *heavenly man;* you have been given the glory and power of God. The book of Romans tells us that God does not show favoritism and this means that everything that has been given to Jesus has also been given to all who believe! Your Father is proud of you, He dearly loves you and when you begin to see yourself in the same way that He sees you, everything in your life will change! My friend, you are accepted and born again, blessed and crowned in glory. You are seated in heavenly places with Christ, and your born again experience begins in the victory of Jesus. Your beginning is the Lord's triumph and your start is His mastery! The savior of the world is no longer the begotten Son of God, but He is now the first-born of many, and many to come!

Chapter 7

# Righteousness and Standing Firm

I deeply desire to help you cultivate a walk with the Lord that will enable you to rise above every trouble and trial. The life that God has purposed for you is close within reach, and every doubt and fear and chain will fall away when you begin to walk in this truth. There is a doorway that will lead you into intimacy with the Lord. It will free you from much bondage and radically change your life. It is called righteousness! Romans 14:17 (NIV) tells us that *"The kingdom of God is...righteousness, peace and joy in the Holy Spirit."* Even if you have sung these words in a song or read them a thousand times throughout your life, I would like you to see them differently. When Paul says that the kingdom is righteousness, peace, and joy, he is describing an order and a pathway. Righteousness will lead you to peace and from there it will lead to joy. What a magnificent gift from the Lord

> There is a doorway that will lead you into intimacy with the Lord. It will free you from much bondage and radically change your life. It is called righteousness!

## The Firm Foundation

When the Lord declares you righteous, a peace that surpasses all understanding will follow; a peace that comes only from Jesus Christ will become your portion! It's important that you understand the true meaning of peace, or "shalom.". Shalom means "wholesome life." It means to be totally and completely alive without any brokenness or defect, a life in which nothing is missing or disturbed! This is the life that God has purposed for you: whole, perfect, and complete. Righteousness leads to peace, but it does not stop there. Righteousness also leads you into joy in the Holy Spirit! The joy of the Lord is your strength! The joy of the Lord prepares you to defend against the enemy and it strengthens you when you are weak. In such a state of peace and joy, great victory is sure to follow. You will walk in victory in your mind, your relationships, your circumstances, and your trials as soon as you understand and embrace the righteousness of the Lord.

Righteousness is when God finds peace with you. It is when you are in right standing with God and He declares you righteous. You see, when God unites with a person He accepts the person exactly as they are. The Lord, after finding no defect or failure in that person, will then declare that they are in right standing with Him. God has declared you righteous because of His son and this is a gift greater than anyone could imagine.

The psalmist declares, *"Enter his gates with thanksgiving and his courts with praise"* (Psalms 100:5 NIV). This is the way in which you are to enter into the presence of God, and once you enter in, you will find righteousness! In the presence of God your life will be saturated with His love and He will write upon your head *"Righteous unto me."* As you go deeper into the presence of the Lord you will find peace and a life untouched by fault or corruption. My friend, as you go even further into the arms of the Lord you will find joy, and it is there where you will be strengthened! It is only in the Lord's presence that you can truly be whole, untouched by the stain of this world and your old self.

There is no doubt that the enemy will begin to attack you as you arise and walk in your freedom. The enemy, however, is nothing to fear. . When a religious voice claims that you must qualify for God's love and benefits, you must no longer receive this. The Kingdom of God does not require you to qualify yourself, rather the Lord is the one who qualifies you, and He does this freely and generously! The bible says in Psalms 65:4 (NKJV), *"Blessed is the man You choose, And cause to approach You."* Not only have you already been qualified, but you are also blessed and fully chosen by God. The Lord does not call you close to Him in order to judge you. He does not call you close in order to punish or destroy you, but He calls you to His side so that He can declare you righteous. He does this so that He can become one spirit with you. When you draw close to the Lord you will see His unfailing grace, His steadfast love, His gift of righteousness, and you will be empowered to live your life abundantly. I so wish that Adam knew it, then rather than hiding from Him he would run in the Father's loving arms and be restored.

## Established and Preserved

The first blessing that you will receive as you walk in righteousness is you will be established! Your feet will be set on solid ground in every relationship and circumstance that you are in. In Isaiah 54:14 (ESV) it is stated clearly, *"In righteousness you shall be established; you shall be far from oppression, for you shall not fear; and from terror, for it shall not come near you."* If you are struggling in any area of your life with instability and inconsistency, my friend, walk into the Lord's presence and receive His declaration over your life. Jesus Christ calls you righteous and this will change and influence every single part of your life. When you introduce righteousness into your life there will be no more wandering and unreliability because you will be grounded in the Lord.

*"You will be established in righteousness and you will be far from oppression, you shall not fear!"* As you walk righteously the enemy will no longer be able to touch you or oppress you. We are created to go from glory to glory. The Lord has not destined us to live in bondage and sinking sand. The Lord declares, *"I know the thoughts that I think toward you, thoughts of peace and not evil, to give you a future and a hope"* (Jeremiah 29:11 NKJV). Hope and peace are His thoughts toward you. Isaiah wrote that you shall be *far from oppression* and *you shall not fear*. If fear has dominated any part of your mind in any circumstance, you must understand that this is not the will of God.

There are many things that you may be prone to fearing. The news is riddled with terror and the world is filled with darkness. Insurance companies use trepidation in all of their advertisements in order to grow their business. We are given many opportunities to be afraid, but this is not our inheritance! The bible declares that the righteous will not be afraid of the sudden fear that comes their way! There is a confidence that comes with righteous living, knowing that you are not alone, knowing that you are fully protected and preserved by God. Isaiah 54:14 does not stop after saying that *"you shall not fear."* This verse goes on to tell us an extraordinary truth, it says, *"Terror shall not come near you!"* My friend, when you live in right standing with God you will walk under His provision and protection.

When you begin to walk in righteousness you will experience a blessing like you have never experienced before. We are told in Deuteronomy 32:4 that our God is without injustice, we are told that He is upright and *righteous*. Righteousness is a part of God's character; there is no evil or darkness in the God in whom we serve. When heaven sees you walk and abide in the nature of God, all of heaven begins working for you. Heaven itself begins to bless and assist you.

It is easy to believe in a God that you know very little about, but many twisted beliefs arise from such a state. No one can fully love something that they do not truly know. As you draw closer to the Lord you will begin to learn more and more about Him. One of the great qualities of God is He is righteous. *"The Lord is righteous in all his ways"* (Psalms 145:17 NIV). If you examine the life of Christ you will learn that He is completely righteous. Jesus was taken to seven different courts and was proven to be blameless. Jesus' enemies could find no fault in Him, nor could His friends; no woman or man could call Him guilty! The Lord is not capricious, He is not only righteous when He is in a good mood. He is righteous in *all* His ways! Now, whatever you are worshiping will begin to become a part of you and you will see its same characteristics within yourself. When you begin to worship Jesus, you begin to reflect Him! Whatever you worship, whatever you behold, it is that very thing in which you will become.

There is no one like our God. He is pure, He is holy, He is righteous and He delights in making you righteous. When you come to Jesus, He does something miraculous. He redeems all of your unrighteousness and He makes you righteous like He is righteous. He clothes you in His very own righteousness and His nature will dominate and shape your life. When you allow the righteousness of God to become part of your life, you will never be the same again. In all your ways, God is calling you to be righteous because He is righteous.

I would like you to understand something about righteousness - righteousness is a lifestyle. Our God is righteous in all His ways, He is faithful in everything, meaning righteousness is *His* lifestyle. God is inviting you and I to participate in His righteousness. God desires to share His attributes with you. Righteousness is an attribute of the holy God and as you behold Him, as you worship Him, He will transform you and you will become righteous, as He is righteous.

Being that righteousness is an attribute of God the very heavens recognize it, this means that blessings are attached to it. My friend, I would like you to understand something especially important. The enemy has no weapon, no temptation, and no assault tactic that could ever overcome the nature of God. This is why the enemy cannot oppress those who walk righteously; this is why the righteous *shall not fear*! The devil has no weapon that could destroy the character of God; our foe has no power that could stand against the divine nature of our Lord.

## Ruling and Reigning

The book of Romans tells us that we must let righteousness train us. I would like to explain to you how this is able to be achieved. First, you must subject every thought to the higher mind of righteousness, or the mind of Christ. If you are tempted or confused, do not rely on your own understanding but simply hand over every thought to the Lord. All struggle and difficulty, every pain, fear and temptation will bow down at the feet of the Lord as you offer it up to Him. The Lord is a wonderful counselor and He will begin to teach you His wonderful nature. As you begin to understand the character of the Lord you will be able to reject anything that isn't of Him. The Holy Spirit and the Word of God is what guides you, it is what enables you to be an overcomer. When you apply this to the places of your life where you struggle and where you feel held captive, the Lord will begin to break off every chain. The feelings that pull you into a downward spiral and the thoughts that seem impossible to fight against will fall under the authority of the nature of God. The emotions that overwhelm you and the cycles that appear to never end will recognize the character of God and fall in alignment with His will. When you accept the righteousness of the Lord you will fulfill the scripture found in Romans 5:17-18, *"Those who are trained by righteousness will rule and reign in their life."* If you let righteousness guide you, you will *rule and reign in your life*. You will be set free and you will be an overcomer in everything that you face!

> **If you let righteousness guide you, you will rule and reign in your life.**

In the Bible when Joseph was still a slave he was called righteous, but he did not stay in his prison. The Lord recognized the righteousness in Joseph; the Lord saw that Joseph was in right standing with Him. Joseph was called out of his bondage and was then exalted by the Lord to become a ruler over Egypt! Daniel was another man in the Bible who found himself in captivity and not just that, Daniel also found himself in a den of lions! Daniel, however, was a righteous man. The Lord found Daniel in right standing with Him and so God did not leave Daniel in chains. The Lord lifted this righteous man out of his situation

> **To live righteously is simply to live like Jesus lived.**

and Daniel became God's royal spokesman in the house of the king. My friend, let me assure you of one thing: I have never seen a righteous man deprived of a promotion in my life. To live righteously is simply to live like Jesus lived. You and I are called to live a holy and blameless life and we are called to be righteous and pleasing to God, but not because it is a religious duty. We are able to delight in righteousness because it is a gift handed to us by God and because it is His nature and in turn, our nature. When you receive the gift of righteousness from the Lord, you will truly be set free and lifted out of any circumstance that imprisons you. When you receive the gift of righteousness from the Lord you will truly be enabled to rule and reign over your life.

You will receive many personal victories from walking righteously, but this is not the only place that you will see benefited. There is also a national blessing for the righteous! God will not only have mercy and favor on you because of your righteousness, but also on your family, in your community and in your country. In Genesis 18, God spoke to Abraham and informed him of the destruction that was going to come upon Sodom and Gomorrah. Abraham, upon the news, began to intercede asking the Lord if He would spare the city if there were fifty righteous people within it. The Lord told Abraham that He would spare the city for the sake of those fifty righteous people. Abraham then lowered the number to forty, thirty, twenty, and finally ten, and the Lord said He would spare the entire city for the sake of the ten righteous. Righteousness influences everything around you: your home and family, your friends and coworkers, the places you travel and the church you attend. One believer choosing to walk in righteousness and receiving this precious gift will spare and impact every life around them! Proverbs 14:34 (NIV)

> God will not only have mercy and favor on you because of your righteousness, but also on your family, in your community and in your country.

states, *"Righteousness exalts a nation, but sin condemns every people."* It's amazing to know that when I allow righteousness to guide my steps and define my life, when I allow righteousness to dominate my thinking and speaking and govern my doing, something incredible will happen. Not only will I be blessed personally but my nation, city, community, and family will be blessed as well! Hallelujah!

God is calling you to be a blesser. You are not called only to reign and rule in your own life, but you are called also to be the reason for freedom in the life of someone else. God is looking for righteousness to be found in His people so that because of His people He can extend His mercy on someone else. The benefits of the righteous ones is that they will not fear, rather they will be established and they will rule and reign in their lives. If you are hindered by fear or tossed mercilessly on wavering ground, if you are being held captive in the kingdom in which you are called to rule over, then it is time to overcome! It is time to stand up and receive the gift of righteousness. It is time to walk in the nature of God.

My friend, courage is your portion. Steadfastness is your portion. Freedom is your portion. A God fearing nation is your portion! Surrender your life, your thoughts, and your ways to Jesus and watch Him transform every piece. The righteousness of one man saved and cleaned the whole world for eternity and He is offering that same gift to you today. *"In righteousness you will be established, you shall be far from oppression, for you shall not fear; and from terror for it shall not come near to you."* This is a promise from the Lord, a promise of protection, of victory, and freedom. You have been established in righteousness, now it is time to walk in the free gift that has been fully paid for by our Lord and savior. It is time to live like Jesus!

Chapter 8

# Righteousness and Our Inheritance

Righteousness by definition means right standing with God. It is to walk intimately and closely with the Lord. Anything that hinders you from coming into the presence of God is keeping you from walking in righteousness whether it is a repeated sin, a painful memory, or an unresolved conflict. It is never worth the distance that it puts in your relationship with the Lord. If you are deprived of joy and desperate for peace this is also a sign that something is wrong. Whatever the barrier may be, it is important to evaluate yourself and remove anything that is pulling you away from the Father. The blessings of righteousness are priceless in value and the Lord is calling you to come close and live in victory. The Lord is calling you to lay down any hindrance and walk worthy of your calling! The Kingdom of God is peace, joy, and righteousness and each of these are gifts that Jesus paid for on the cross. The enemy has lost the right to steal these gifts from us. You no longer have to live lacking joy, peace, and righteousness. It is time that each of us begin to receive the glorious life in which the Lord is offering to us!

## Hindrances

Doubt is a terrible hindrance and can often be overlooked, but to walk in doubt is to walk in unrighteousness. In Romans 14:23 (NIV) we are told, *"But whoever has doubts is condemned if they eat, because their eating is not from faith; and everything that does not come from faith is sin."* This verse speaks to the importance of faith even in something as seemingly insignificant as eating. Faith is extremely important and every believer is called out of disbelief and into a life of faith.

We are told of another sin in the book of James 4:17 (NIV) where it says, *"If anyone, then, knows the good they ought to do and doesn't do it, it is sin for them."* When you know what is right and you choose what is wrong it is sinful and those who live in this manner have chosen unrighteousness. Before we move any further, I would like you to understand that there are two different kinds of sins. There is a sin that leads to death and a sin that is merely a hindrance. We are made aware of this in 1 John 5:16 (ESV) that, *"If anyone sees his brother committing a sin not leading to death, he shall ask, and God will give him life—to those who commit sins that do not lead to death. There is sin that leads to death; I do not say that one should pray for that."* The Lord is calling every believer to be free from both kinds of sin, whether big or small. All sin is unrighteousness and both kinds of sin will lead to a fractured relationship with the Lord.

Of the two different kinds of sins mentioned above, one is of doubt and disbelief and the other is of doing that which is wrong in spite of knowing what is right. To live in doubt and disbelief is to not lay faith down as the foundation, therefore living under religion and the law. Living under the yoke of the law nullifies the blood and sacrifice of Jesus. Religion uproots our hope from the soil of the victory of Jesus Christ and transplants it into the dry and cracked ground of our own doings where nothing can survive. All hope wilts when we put it into our own works.

Then there is the sin of knowing what is right and choosing to do what is wrong. This could be as simple as caring for your animal as we are told in Proverbs 12:10 (NIV) that, *"The righteous care for the needs of their animals."* There is a conversation between Jesus and Peter that is recorded in the book of John where Jesus asks Peter a question. Jesus asks Peter if he loves Him. Peter responds that certainly he does and Jesus replies, *"Then feed my sheep."* Now, of course Jesus is not speaking of literal sheep, rather He is speaking of people, but there is still something important to note here. In Proverbs we hear that the righteous man cares for something even as small as an animal. In the book of John, Jesus says that if Peter loves Him he must care for the sheep. In this we can see clearly that the righteous person who loves the Lord is caring and loving toward others. There is no selfishness in the kingdom of God and if there is any selfishness within us or if we are not caring for those around us then we are not walking in righteousness. Those who live righteously are filled with joy and peace, and they are enriched by faith and care. The righteous are known by their integrity and character, and my friend, the blessings of righteousness are many. The blessings of righteousness come from the Lord Himself and never fail or fall short; they never perish or succumb to decay!

**The Blessings of Righteousness**

There is a blessing given to those who are righteous; a truly remarkable blessing from God. Righteousness guarantees our prayers to be answered! Everyone longs for their prayers to be answered but James 5:17 (NKJV) tells us that, *"The effective, fervent prayer of a righteous man avails much."* The Bible proves that God has tremendous respect for the prayer of a righteous person. Some people pray and find no response while another person prays and everything shifts at the sound of their voice. Daniel in the Bible prayed and his prayers tamed lions, while his enemies prayed to no avail. Elijah prayed and fire came down from heaven, while the Baal worshipers prayed and were left mortified. Peter prayed and a lame man could arise and walk, while others could only stand in awe. This is what happens when a righteous person prays:, the Lord is obliged to answer. Many people travel far and wide seeking famous men and women of God to pray for them. People seek such names because they have seen God do mighty things through those men and women. The only difference, however, between that mighty man or woman and any other ordinary Christian is that they are walking in righteousness with God. There is a confidence and a faith that comes with righteousness, and when your confidence is shaken it is always linked to your walk with God. When one steps into unrighteousness all confidence shatters and fear sets in, a fear that God will not answer the prayer or plea. When one is walking in righteousness

> The prayers of the righteous are effective.

a confidence and trust concretes within and there is an assurance that God will honor His righteous friends. There is a covenant between a righteous person and God, assuring the righteous one that his prayers will always be answered. The prayers of the righteous are effective. When a righteous person prays God will not reject it, He will not delay it, He will not ignore it.

There is another blessing that is lavished upon those who walk in right standing with God. Proverbs 21:21 states, *"Whoever pursues righteousness and love will find life, prosperity and honor."* Everyperson who walks this earth aspires to have a good life to some capacity. If one were to reach for a good life, however, and skip righteousness and love, it would be comparable to desiring the fruit without first planting seeds and laying roots. We are also told in this verse that prosperity is a gift for the righteous and godly prosperity is not like that of the worlds. The wealth and success of the world fades and falters; it finds wings and flies away. The unrighteous toil and strive but are left emptier than before, feeble and broken by what they thought would fill them. In fact, Proverbs 13:22 (ISV) tells us that, *"the wealth of the wicked is reserved for the righteous."* Wealth itself knows that its job is to associate with righteousness. The wealth and prosperity of the world isn't real. This is seen clearly in the lives of many rich and successful people who simultaneously live in great turmoil. If you look closely at the lives of the people who the secular world deems as prosperous you will see a lack of peace and joy. The lives of these wealthy people are often filled with pain and dissatisfaction; a spirit of suicide and depression plagues them. There are many who are rich in money but are poor and starved for true meaning and value! My friend, righteousness is the root of a truly blessed life; a life of worth and real prosperity. It is the righteousness of God that leads to joy and peace and honor. Solomon was the wisest man in the world and it was he who wrote, *"Whoever pursues righteousness and love finds life, prosperity and honor"* (Proverbs 21:21 NIV). It is important to ask yourself what you are in pursuit of, because you cannot have the fruit without the root. Life or prosperity without God is not life or prosperity at all, it is empty and meaningless.

## Living from Righteousness

The focus of this entire book has been dedicated to the study of righteousness. Righteousness is the root that produces the fruit of blessing in each of our lives. We live in a society and a generation that moves at a fast pace, and often times we expect God to move at this same pace. Many people desire fast answers to their questions or problems, and many people desire the fruit without first acquiring the root. God does not ask us to be fast paced people, He asks us to be anchored and trustworthy. God calls us to be enduring and rooted! One thing that is so extraordinary about the Lord is that He has been patiently working on your life. The Lord is gently aligning every piece with patient forbearing and expectant love! As you plant your roots in the righteousness of God and truly receive the gift of righteousness then something grand will happen. The fruit of joy will grow and grant you strength, and next the fruit of peace will bloom and make you whole! You, however, cannot have one without the other. You cannot grow the fruit of joy without the root of righteousness. It is easy to chase after peace and joy while refusing to walk in righteousness, because righteousness requires sacrifice. Righteousness requires honoring the Lord and putting Him above the desires of the flesh.

> The heavens shake at the prayer of a righteous person.

    I want to encourage you today, because as you evaluate your life and learn of the righteousness of God you will begin to realize something great. Every victory of Jesus, every success of any famous man or woman of God is within your grasp. The moment that you step into consistency with God and begin to walk in righteousness you will see the gravity that your words carry in heaven. You will see the Lord do even more than you can imagine as you are promised in Ephesians 3:20, *"Now unto him who is able to do exceedingly and abundantly beyond what we could ask or even imagine according to the power that worketh in us."* This means that when you allow the power of God and His righteousness to work inside of you and transform you, your prayer will become exceedingly effective! The heavens shake at the prayer of a righteous person. In the Bible when the apostles would pray the very place in which they stood would shake! People have fasted and prayed for weeks on end only to find themselves discouraged because their prayers were not answered. Before fasting and asking for answers, however, God is calling us to walk righteously and come close to Him. If you are not walking righteously you cannot expect your prayers to be answered.

Psalms 50:16 (NIV) proclaims, *"But to the wicked person, God says: 'What right have you to recite my laws or take my covenant on your lips?'"* God has inclined His ears to His righteous ones and He is pleased to hear them call on His name! We have a provision of mercy made available to us so that we may no longer continue to walk unrighteously, but instead be transformed as the sons and daughters of most High God, walking in His divine nature. This is why John 1:12 (NKJV) plainly states, *"But as many as received Him, to them He gave the right to become children of God, to those who believe in His name."*

I want you to understand that God loves righteousness. It is His divine nature and when He sees His children walking in His nature it pleases Him dearly! The Lord blesses the righteous and finds delight within them. Prosperity and a good life require an environment of righteousness. When you are rooted and grounded in righteousness you will then produce the fruit of success, fulfillment, and a good life! This is why righteousness is so important, it is the foundation in which everything lasting is built upon. Righteousness will transform our modern churches and culture; it will radically influence our schools and society! Every life that is grounded in righteousness is sure to explode in blessings of joy and peace and success! I have studied righteousness for some time now and I am yet to find anything negative attached to it. You will never be lost if you make righteousness your friend There is even a path made just for the righteous! The prophet Isaiah said that there is path in which there is no sorrow, a path in which there is no pain, a path where everything blossoms, a path of blessing and prosperity. On this path no wicked will walk, only the righteous. It is laid aside and preserved for those in right standing with God. Proverbs 4:18 (NLT) tells us, *"The way of the righteous is like the first gleam of dawn, which shines ever brighter until the full light of day."*

I would like to clarify to you that you are not being called into a life of righteous acts and religious doings. Righteousness is not about what you do, righteousness is about who you are! People can act righteous, just as demons can appear as angels, but the Lord desires to transform you. The moment that you step into righteousness you also step into the nature of God and then honor will follow you, prosperity will find you, and true life will be your portion!

> Righteousness is not about what you do, righteousness is about who you are!

There was a time in my life when I was working for a Christian television program. I was the manager and there were people who were under my authority. I found that those who I was leading were not honoring me and this was deeply concerning. I was trying to decide how to address the situation when the Lord spoke to me: *"Pursue righteousness and honor will attach itself to you."* So I set my heart to pursue righteousness. I dealt fairly with every individual; I began speaking with them and intentionally getting to know every one of them. I did not allow my wounds and hurts to change the way I saw each person and I did not let the insults or behaviors of others change the way I lived. My friend, when I began to pursue righteousness something incredible happened. The culture of that entire organization began to shift, and a lifestyle of honor formed in our midst! When you run after the Lord and His righteousness, blessings and gifts are the result and the fruit.

Jesus spoke in Matthew 6:33 (KJV) saying, *"Seek ye first the kingdom of God, and his righteousness; and all these things shall be added unto you."* Just before this verse Jesus directed us to never worry about tomorrow and He assured us that we do not have to live in fear or anxiety. Jesus instructed us not to dwell on what we will eat, or drink, or wear, and He gave us the key to acquiring a blessed life. "Seek first the kingdom of God and His righteousness and all these things will be added!" Something important to note is that Jesus did not say seek your own righteousness, He said seek *His* righteousness. This is referring to the righteousness of God. In this we know that we are not required to fake or forge our own righteousness, but rather to let the Lord transform us into His nature and character! When God transforms you, righteousness will become your default; the way you think, act, and speak will be in tune with Christ! The way you feel things will change and the way you see the world will never be the same. If you are troubled by any worry or fear, if the future is daunting and you feel trapped, then it is time to turn to the Lord and seek His kingdom and His righteousness first. When you seek righteousness you will surely be set free from every fear of tomorrow. When you seek righteousness, honor and prosperity will find you. When you seek righteousness all of heaven will fight on your behalf!

The righteousness of the Lord is a gift that must be received in faith. I would like you to recall the parable of the prodigal son. In this story the youngest son found himself in a terrible situation due to very poor decisions. The prodigal son had lost his prosperity and his way of life; he had lost his honor and he was poor and alone. The son traveled home in hopes to be a servant in the house of his father, but the father had quite a different plan. When the father saw his prodigal son he restored him to honor and prosperity, he gave his son everything that he had lost in his rebellion. Nobody could condemn the son because the father had forgiven him; no one could accuse his son because the father had accepted him. No one could even catch the son because the father was the first to run to him! Our heavenly Father does the same thing for us: before anyone can even touch us, He bestows His righteousness on us. David said in Psalm 32, "Blessed is the man whose sins you do not remember, whose transgressions you have removed, whose iniquities you have forgiven." In the days of David it was not thought to be possible for sin to be forgotten. So, when David said in this same chapter "blessed is the generation whose sin is not taken into account by God," he was speaking of a gift. The gift of righteousness is given to us the moment that we believe, but it is from there that we get to choose to live righteously everyday. My friend, when you know the Lord you will not live righteously in order to receive a blessing. When you see how the Lord has loved you, accepted you, and lavished you with His blessings, your righteousness will be a reaction; a response to beholding Him! Your choices will then be defined by Christ who lives within you. The Bible commands in Romans 6:11, *"Consider yourself dead to sin and alive to righteousness."* You are reborn into the righteous nature of God your Father!

Out of your being comes your doing, and in this you can rest assured that when Christ begins living inside of you it is He who commands your actions. This is why Romans 6 (NIV) describes something amazing to us when it says,

> *"In the same way, count yourselves dead to sin but alive to God in Christ Jesus. Therefore do not let sin reign in your mortal body so that you obey its evil desires. Do not offer any part of yourself to sin as an instrument of wickedness, but rather offer yourselves to God as those who have been brought from death to life; and offer every part of yourself to him as an instrument of righteousness. For sin shall no longer be your master, because you are not under the law, but under grace. So let it be the same way with you. Since you're now joined with Him you must continually view yourself as dead and unresponsive to sins appealing."*

It is not you staying away from sin that makes you one with God. On the contrary, you are one with God and therefore you are made able to stay away from sin. It is by your union with Jesus Christ that you can be righteous and in turn, be an overcomer in every situation.

As this belief system takes root in your heart, your ability to resist sin and its appeal will grow. You will begin to choose what brings joy to the Lord and you will see His favor and goodness expressed within every situation. When you lay yourself down and let Christ live within you, He begins to act through you! You must continually submit to Him and let yourself become dead and unresponsive to sin and fleshliness. Your life as a Christian is meant to be dependent on the Lord. He does not call you to bear anything alone. Jesus said in Matthew 11:30 (NIV), "*My yoke is easy and my burden is light.*" The Lord did not give you life so that you could follow rules and learn to rely on your works. The Lord *is* life Himself and He comes into you, works through you and His nature grows from within you.

Jesus stood before a four-day-old tomb where his friend had been laid and He spoke to the Father. "*I thank you, you always hear me. I do this so that they may know that you've sent me*" (John 11:42). After Jesus said this, He called to Lazarus and He brought his friend back from the dead. A righteous man is confident in the face of death, in the face of calamity and in the face of despair! As you walk righteously there is a confidence like no other that will fill your heart.

If you are wondering how to pursue righteousness, I will put it quite simply: all you must do is pursue Jesus! If at times you stumble and fall and your heart tells you that you are no longer righteous, you can overcome this lie with the truth. Your righteousness does not come from yourself, your righteousness comes from Christ as a free gift. If you fall down seven times your savior's hand is outstretched to you and He will never leave you on the

> Your righteousness does not come from yourself, your righteousness comes from Christ as a free gift.

ground. As stated at the beginning of this chapter, righteousness by definition means "right standing with God" and in this you can be sure that your righteousness is never compromised. You are fully accepted and outrageously loved by your Father. He has declared you righteous and now it is simply time to walk in His nature. It is time to live from your spirit and train your mind to accept the gifts and promises of the Lord.

If you make your source anything but Jesus it will result in instability and turmoil. An urge to perform and a sense of unworthiness is often present. My friend, Jesus must be your source. When He becomes your source, your character will be transformed and renewed. When Jesus becomes your only source, blessings and prosperity will overflow from a place of rest and peace! Jesus stated that He only did what He saw the Father do, and this is how we are to live also. As Christians we should not do what is right in order to be approved or accepted by God. We are already His, He is already ours, and because of this our behavior will change and shape into His behavior and character. Our very DNA is radically transformed by our Father. We can rest and receive every promise that God has made available for His children! Joy, peace, prosperity, honor, life, rest, strength, confidence, and the list goes on! Every blessing is your inheritance. Let the Father refine your nature and shape your DNA, and you will begin living from His works and His righteousness!

## Chapter 9

# Righteousness and the Nature of Blessings

Many people live their life searching for blessings. I have seen men and women travel far and wide to receive a blessing or escape a curse. Sometimes people will rush to famous preachers in order to receive prayer and freedom. The blessings that come from people, however, cannot last. The high wears off, the chains feel tighter, and these people find themselves in the same wearisome position as before. When this happens they will get up and chase after another church or preacher, until once again they are back to square one. I have seen people destroy their lives simply because they sought blessings in the wrong places. You see, these people in search of blessings will receive prayer from anointed pastors and prophets, and oftentimes they will be granted blessings. Though these people will be blessed for a time, their hearts do not change and in turn the cycle will restart and the hardships will reset. Blessings are not a coincidence; blessings are not a product of sheer luck. In fact, blessings have a nature and they are cultivated in very specific soil. King Solomon was the wisest man on earth and he wrote the words, in Proverbs 10:6 (NKJV) *"Many blessings are on the head of the righteous."* Blessings have a nature and that nature is righteousness.

Jesus sent seventy of His disciples into various towns and villages and before they departed He gave them clear instructions. Jesus told His disciples that they should stay in any home that accepts them. He commanded that they should release a blessing on the place in which they stay. Jesus said that if the house is worthy of the blessing it will remain there, and if not, it will return to where it came from. Like a helicopter or a plane, a blessing requires a landing pad, airport, similarly there is only one place where blessings can stay and abide. On the head of the righteous is where blessings grow; it is where blessings land and remain. The Bible is clear that if you are righteous, you will not have to beg for blessings. Instead of being starved for them, they will land and attach themselves to you. Paul wrote to the church of Ephesus saying that "every blessing has already been given to us in Christ" (Ephesians 1:3). If you are not beholding blessings in any area of your life, then there is something that you must seek. Before asking for healing, or freedom, or success in this sphere of your life, ask the Lord for righteousness. Turn from any ungodliness, become righteous in your ways, and the soil of any situation will bear the fruit of innumerable blessings! When you apply righteousness to your life you will no longer have the need to ask for blessings, because blessings are a by-product of righteousness.

Often I hear people lament over their situations saying that they tithe and yet they are still in debt. People say that they pray but their family is still in shambles, or that they worship and yet are not free. I think many people forget that Jesus spoke these words in Matthew 6:33 (ESV): *"But seek first the kingdom of God and his righteousness, and all these things will be added to you."*

It is important to realize that your lifestyle affects your offering. Cain and Abel both brought the Lord an offering, but only one pleased Him. Your presentation and offering is not what grows blessings, it is your heart and lifestyle that matter to God. During the revival in Samaria a former sorcerer named Simon saw the works of the Holy Spirit through Paul and the apostles. Simon had become a follower of Christ, but when he saw the works of the Holy Spirit he wanted to buy it. Paul rebuked Simon saying, *"Your money perish with you, because you thought that the gift of God could be purchased with money"* (Acts 8:20 NKJV). Simon's mentality is actually quite common within the modern church. It is the mentality that you can bypass the spiritual process and giving a perishable offering in order to receive something from God. People will invest into a church, feed the poor, and tithe ten percent all in an effort to produce a fruit without ever even planting something. You have to understand that it is not what you are offering that produces a harvest, it is indeed the condition of your heart! Even one step that you take in righteousness will be blessed and multiplied by the Lord. As you walk righteously you will be blessed wherever you go, in whatever you do, and whenever you speak. Your prayers will shake the earth and the heavens; you will be honored and you will prosper in your life. Whatever you do, do it in righteousness and you will be grounded and established, you will not be shaken. The world often tries to tell you that you must become cunning and wicked to achieve success, but blessings cannot grow in such soil. Jesus spoke these words in Matthew 16:26: *"Oh foolish man how will it benefit you if you gain the world and lose your own very soul."* My friend, examine your ways. Let righteousness reign within the greatest and smallest areas of your life. Anything that is sown outside the realm of righteousness will wither away; it is temporary and cannot last. The world may market luxury, but like a futile breath it evaporates in the air. Every blessing that sprouts up from righteous soil, however, will remain forever. It will not fade or fester like that of the world. Solomon wrote in Proverbs 10:22 (NLT): *"The blessing of the LORD makes a person rich, and he adds no sorrow with it."* The world blesses only to destroy you, but when the Lord blesses, He protects you.

When God blesses you, there will be no fear of losing what you have, and you will be confident that His glory will flow into every circumstance! Proverbs 28:1 (ESV) states: *"The righteous are bold as a lion."* A while back my family and I had the pleasure of going on a safari. As we drove through wild terrain I was startled when my gaze was suddenly met by a tiger. The tiger stood only ten feet away from me and I remember quite clearly the details of his posture. He was majestic; his eyes were filled to the brim with the utmost power. All that the tiger had to do was look at me and I began to tremble from head to toe! This fearless beast walked in daring courage and Proverbs compares the righteous to such creatures. Righteousness strips away all fear and timidity; the righteous are as bold as lions!

The reason that the righteous can be as bold as a lion in every trial and hardship that they face is because they have a deliverer! *"The righteous person may have many troubles, but the Lord delivers him from all of them"* (Psalms 34:19 NIV).

This is yet another blessing for those who walk righteously: they are guaranteed deliverance! Every person in the Bible who was declared righteous by the Lord ended up in a difficult situation, but they were never left there. In the story of Joseph, a righteous man, we see the Lord's deliverance first hand. Joseph was sold into slavery by his jealous brothers, but the Lord rescued him and gave him favor and authority in Egypt. Joseph was then framed for a horrible crime that he had taken no part of, and was sentenced to prison. God did not leave Joseph in the dungeon; the Lord delivered Joseph from his desperate condition and restored him to prosperity. Joseph became a ruler in Egypt and a blessing to his family for many generations to follow. A righteous man named Daniel was sent to the lion's den because he would not cease from praying to the Lord. God did not forsake Daniel in this hour. Instead, the angel of the Lord shut the mouths of the lions and delivered Daniel from his tribulations! Noah was another righteous man of God and he lived during a dark age. The Lord ordered a flood to destroy all of mankind, all except for one righteous man: Noah. Noah and his entire family were spared. God delivered them from the flood and chose to never flood the earth again. Joseph and Mary were righteous in the Lord's eyes and when Jesus was given to them as a baby they faced a daunting trial. King Herod ordered a widespread massacre of children. Before the slaughter could even take place an angel warned Joseph in a dream and the family was brought to safety. You see, all of these righteous people faced treacherous situations but God delivered them and their families out of every one of them! God delivers the righteous, and though they will face troubles, they will never be overcome by them.

Fear grips our nation. We see this clearly in the anxiety that is tormenting our society. There is only one answer to this problem. The answer is not antidepressants, or therapy, or entertainment. The answer is the gift that the Lord has given to us and that is His very own righteousness! This boldness and peace will surpass understanding; it will help you in the darkest of times.

When Covid swept through the world fear was very prevalent. India was hit incredibly hard by this great devastation: there were deaths by the millions, mass burials, and people isolated in their homes. The streets and shops were empty while countless individuals sunk into a terrible pit of fear. I turned to the Lord during this time and He reminded me of the truth that *"the righteous are as bold as lions!"* In that very moment all fear of sickness left me and something shifted inside of me. I began to see the pandemic as an opportunity for God to use my life. Every place within my heart that was once weighed down with fear was now elevated with faith! As Covid continued to run rampant some close friends and I were able to provide food for the people in our neighborhood. We supplied groceries and medicine to those in need and we did this almost everyday. I was often in close proximity with many sick people. I took countless of them to the hospital but I was never infected! I write this to encourage you that you can be bold and without fear in every situation. The righteous are as bold as lions. This means when troubling news comes to you, when fear lurks and rises against you, you shall not be afraid.

In the Bible we see the entire nation of Israel frantic with terror when they are met by Goliath. The people of Israel would hide themselves and tremble at the giant who opposed their God until a righteous young man appeared. David was young but he was as bold as a lion and the Lord was on his side. David walked into the battle with no armor, defeating and killing Goliath with a stone and nothing more. When you stand on righteous ground the Lord will cover and protect you and fear will not infiltrate your life. When you allow the righteousness of God to fill you it will set you free from every fear. If there is any part of your life that is being ruled by anxiety or fear you must understand that you were created to be an overcomer and a victor in all that you do! This is why the Bible says that the righteous will rule and reign in life. The righteous are as bold as lion.

## Righteousness and Success

There is an ache for success in us all. People go to great lengths and spend exorbitant amounts of money in order to get their kids into prominent colleges. Often the relationships we choose, the places we go, and the things that we fill our calendar with are done with an agenda. We have an agenda for success. While success is not bad, in fact success is Biblical, you must understand that there is a formula for success. Success, like everything in God's kingdom, has a nature and it will grow in the soil of righteousness. Proverbs 2:7 (NIV) reveals this very thing to us when it says, *"He holds success in store for the upright, he is a shield to those whose walk is blameless."* Success is attached to righteousness. When God is working from within you, success will be the outcome.

> Success, like everything in God's kingdom, has a nature and it will grow in the soil of righteousness.

If we again recall the story of Joseph, we see a man who is sold into slavery and at one point thrown into prison. Because of the righteousness of Joseph the Lord granted him success and God promoted him to a powerful position in Egypt. Joseph led the country during a devastating time and brought success to everything he touched. The Bible promises success for the righteous; He guarantees his favor to those who walk in His ways.

When you are walking in righteousness you will begin experiencing breakthrough and success within your finances. *"Now He who supplies seed to the storehouse and bread for food will also supply and increase your store of seed and will enlarge the harvest of your righteousness."* Paul wrote these words in 2 Corinthians 9:10. I want you to understand the process of this financial favor. As you sow into your church and the people around you, and as you give generously, you will be blessed financially. When you sow into God's kingdom, it is counted as an act of righteousness. This is because walking righteously is simply walking in the character of God, and God is a giving God. When you were born into this world you were born into sin; you were born stingy and selfish, but praise God, you have been born again! *"Let him who steals steal no more, rather work from his own hands so that he may have something to give to someone who is in need."* This verse in Ephesians 4:28 is speaking to robbers, but it is a testimony to all. Though you once were selfish and withholding, your DNA is now changing; your heart is being transformed. You see, righteousness is God's nature, and so when we walk in His nature He blesses us. The famous verse, John 3:16 (NIV), says, *"For God so loved the world that He gave..."* Giving is a quality of God and the Lord gives because of love, not obligation. When we are living in generosity and doing so from a place of love, it catches God's attention. God blesses the generous and the righteous; He blesses their storehouses and grants them financial favor!

**Righteousness and Healing**

When you plant one seed of righteousness you do not receive *one* fruit, but rather you receive an overflow of fruit from the Lord! One of the many fruits of righteousness is the fruit of healing. In Malachi 4:2 (NIV) it is written, *"But for you who revere my name, the sun of righteousness will rise with healing in its rays. And you will go out and frolic like well-fed calves."* Healing is guaranteed for those who choose to walk in the ways of the Lord; health will rise up like rays of sunlight on the righteous. The word "disease" comes from the French root word *"dis-ease,"* which means *"a lack of ease."* My friend, the righteous are healed of every physical disease, but also of every mental disease. If there is a physical ailment that causes a lack of ease in your life there is healing in righteousness. If there is a mental ailment such as depression, or sadness, or hopelessness, there is freedom in the righteousness of Jesus Christ! *"Since you love righteousness and you hate wickedness, therefore God; your God has anointed you with the oil of gladness."* This verse is from Psalms 45:7 and it promises gladness! If you are lacking gladness and emptied of your joy, there is a promise of gladness that you must step into. Love righteousness, revere the name of the Lord, and then watch your healing rise and fall on you like streams of water. Watch the Lord anoint your head with gladness like oil! There are promises waiting for the righteous to stand up and walk in; to stand up and walk in the anointing that the Lord has already given to them!

Psalms 34:15 (NIV) states, *"The eyes of the Lord are on the righteous, and his ears are attentive to their cry."* The Creator of heaven and earth pays close attention to the righteous. The eyes of God are searching for one thing: righteousness. We are told in 2 Chronicles 16:9 that, *"The eyes of the Lord look to and fro on the planet earth searching for a person whose heart is loyal to Him so that He can show Himself powerful on behalf of that person."* The Lord is searching and when He finds a loyal and righteous friend He works in support of that person! If you have been abiding by the word of God, if you have been residing in Jesus Christ, if you have been walking in righteousness, don't be discouraged when difficult times happen. You can be sure of one thing: the eyes of the Lord are upon the righteous!

The blessings of righteousness never cease, they only grow brighter and brighter. Proverbs 11:18 (NKJV) tells us that there is something awaiting the righteous! "He who sows righteousness *will have* a sure reward." What this verse is telling us is extraordinary. It is saying that everything that we do out of the character of Jesus Christ will reap a harvest! This verse is promising us that as we walk in the nature of our God we will be rewarded. If you do not sow in the character of God, you cannot reap His reward. If you sow in jealousy you will reap strife, or if you sow in pride you will reap insult. But if you sow in righteousness you will receive a reward from God! My friend, in difficult relationships you must begin to sow righteousness. In strenuous business decisions, begin to sow righteousness. In your finances, and families, and in every broken place in your life, begin sowing righteousness and simply watch everything change! Throughout the Bible we see people who were treated wickedly, but when they responded in righteousness it resulted in God's favor…so it will be for all of us! When Jesus walked the earth He did the Father's will wherever He went, no matter how He was treated or what others said. Jesus never reacted in anger or took revenge on those who opposed Him. Jesus had only one response to those around Him: He demonstrated the Father's perfect love. Our Lord sowed righteousness in every circumstance that He found Himself in and because of this He was rewarded. The reward that God gives is eternal, meaning that it cannot be snatched or broken! Blessings are promised to those who chase after righteousness! Jesus said in Matthew 5:6 (NIV), *"Blessed are those who hunger and thirst for righteousness."* The Lord is not telling us to pursue success, or healing, or popularity. He said *"hunger and thirst for righteousness."*

The Bible discloses to us that in the last days there will be those who hate righteousness and love self. There will be people who will live their lives strictly to please themselves. The wicked, however, will not prosper. Their pleasure will disappear in their hands while the blessings of the righteous will never end! The Prophet Jeremiah cried out to the Lord and asked Him an important question, "Why does the way of the wicked prosper? Why do all the faithless live at ease?" (Jeremiah 12:1 NIV). It is amazing that Jeremiah asked this question, because there will be times in our lives where it seems that way. Even prophet Habakkuk, struggled with this same quest however, he reaches a compelling conclusion and ends his book with these words,

> *"Though the fig tree may not blossom, nor fruit be on the vines; though the labor of the olive may fail, and the fields yield no food; Though the flocks may be cut off from the fold, And there be no herd in the stalls- Yet I will rejoice in the Lord, I will joy in the Lord of my salvation. The Lord God is my strength; He will make my feet like the deer's feet, and He will make me walk on high hills."*

Habakkuk concluded that all else is temporary and fading, all except for the Lord. Habakkuk decided that God Himself was the reward of the righteous. This prophet knew that all who are wicked will end in destruction, but the righteous will end in glory.

Righteousness surpasses every treasure in value; nothing can compare to its worth. Proverbs 11:4 (TPT) reveals something truly significant: *"When judgment day comes, all the wealth of the world won't help you one bit, so be rich in righteousness for that's the only thing that can save you in death."* If you have been abiding in Jesus Christ and walking in His ways, if you have been growing in intimacy with God and receiving the gift of righteousness, be sure of one thing: your problems will never overpower you, you will always have victory in your life, you will see great things and you will not be put to shame. No matter how many trials come your way you must not be discouraged. The Lord will set a table for you in the presence of your enemies. David said in Psalms 41:11 (NKJV), *"By this I know that You are well pleased with me, Because my enemy does not triumph over me."* The Lord works on behalf of the righteous; they please Him and He will never let them be overcome by evil. Psalms 55:22 (NIV) declares, *"Cast your cares on the LORD and he will sustain you; he will never let the righteous be shaken."* This is a glorious promise! No matter what happens in your life, if you are righteous in the sight of the Lord He will never let you be shaken. The Lord takes personal interest in perfecting you and securing you. When the storm comes it may uproot everything around you, but it will not be able to touch you. The Bible says in Psalms 91:10 (NASB) that, *"Nor will any plague come near your tent."* The Lord is a fortress to the righteous; a shield of protection around them! What is there left to fear when God is on your side!

Wherever there is a righteous person, God cannot help but get involved. He cannot leave the situation alone! Wherever the righteous go, God will follow; wherever they stay, God is right there beside them. Psalms 37 (TPT) states, *"It is much better to have little combined with much of God than to have the fabulous wealth of the wicked and nothing else. For the Lord takes care of all his forgiven ones while the strength of evil men will surely slip away."* There is another verse that says, *"The Lord upholds the righteous"* (Psalms 37:17 NIV). This means that when waters rise and troubles surround, the Lord will lift you out of their reach. God is not saying that He is sending His angels to lift you up and save you, what God is saying is that He Himself will uphold and protect His righteous ones!

I want you to know that these incredible rewards and blessings are reserved for the righteous. Righteousness is not striving for perfection. Righteousness is simply walking with Jesus; it is a close and beautiful relationship with the Lord. All these eternal blessings only increase as you continue to learn that He is changing your DNA and His nature is now your nature. When I first began studying righteousness I was truly amazed at how great a gift it really is. The Lord has made a way so that each of us can walk in constant blessing. Many will submit to fear when great darkness falls over the earth, but not the righteous. Even as Jesus was being crucified He was unshaken. Jesus knew that the Father would not let Him decay in the pit of hell. Jesus knew that the Father would not let a single bone of His be broken. As Jesus took His final breath He spoke out, *"Father, into your hands I commit my spirit"* (Luke 23:46 NIV). Jesus was confident that the Father would never leave the righteous in the darkness; He trusted that God would raise Him from the grave! Jesus prophesied every event leading to His crucifixion before it had even taken place; He was fully reliant on the promises of God. Even when our Lord was only an infant born into a manger, He attracted treasures like gold, myrrh and frankincense!

> Righteousness is simply walking with Jesus; it is a close and beautiful relationship with the Lord.

When Jesus walked the earth He was followed by multitudes; crowds gathered everywhere that He stepped. Jesus is the ultimate blessing! He attracts every other blessing and when you become one with Him nothing can touch you! Psalms 125:4 proclaims, *"Righteousness cannot be defeated."*

I would like to end this chapter by recalling a beautiful story from Matthew 8 (NIV). When Jesus was walking He was met by a man suffering from leprosy. The man called out to Him saying, *"'Lord, if you are willing, you can make me clean.'"* To this Jesus replied, *"I am willing...be clean*!" Jesus touched the man and in a moment the man was made well again; the pain and disease had left him. I would like you to notice something about this encounter: Jesus touched the man, but He did not receive the leprosy. Jesus healed the man, but the disease did not defile Him. Instead, the holiness of the Lord devoured the sickness of the man and he was made pure! When our unrighteousness meets the righteousness of Jesus Christ, we do not make Him dirty, instead, His righteousness engulfs and purifies us. When our darkness meets His light, it exposes and revives all of our dying parts. I pray that as you ponder these words, you would not solely be educated, but your heart would be transformed! Righteousness is a gift that was paid for with the precious blood of the Lord. All you must do is receive this gift; all you must do is come to Jesus and let Him make you clean and whole. When you step into righteousness, you embark on the greatest adventure of your life. When you step into righteousness you make the Lord smile because you are living in *His* nature!

Chapter 10

# Righteousness and the Provision of God

The first time that righteousness is mentioned in the Bible is in Genesis 6:9 (NIV). *"This is the account of Noah and his family. Noah was a righteous man, blameless among the people of his time, and he walked faithfully with God."* Noah was the only righteous man in all of the earth at this time. The world had grown desperately wicked and so the Lord opened the floodgates of heaven and burst forth the springs of the great deep. The flood destroyed all of mankind except for one man and his family. Noah was a man who walked faithfully with God. Noah and his entire family were spared from destruction because of his righteousness. The Lord personally attends to the matters of the righteous. Psalms 37:16 (NIV) tells us, *"Better the little that the righteous have than the wealth of many wicked, for the power of the wicked will be broken but the Lord upholds the righteous."* The Lord is saying through this verse that He will not forsake the righteous; He will never abandon them! Do not forget this promise. When there is a righteous person, God will always work on their behalf. God cannot stay out of the affairs of the righteous. It is time to discover what really happens when God steps into the circumstances of a righteous person.

## When God Steps In

In the book of Daniel there is a story of three young men who are known as Shadrach, Meshach, and Abednego. These three men resisted the order of the king to worship a gold statue and because of their defiance they were sentenced to death. The king ordered the furnace to be increased to seven times the usual heat. We are told that the furnace was so scorching that the guards died instantly when they threw the three men into the fire. Now these three young men were righteous in the Lord's sight and the Lord did not leave them to face the flames alone. Everyone who was present, including the king himself, witnessed a fourth man in the fire! This fourth man was the Son of God and no harm came to the three men in the fire. When Shadrach, Meshach, and Abednego were pulled from the flames, it is said that the only thing that was singed was the ropes that had bound them. My friend, the world may rise against you, but history proves that when God stands in defense of a righteous person no weapon formed against them will prevail.

Righteousness influences and affects everyone who is associated with it. There is a wonderful story in the Bible of a widow who meets the prophet Elijah. The woman told the prophet, *"My husband is dead, he was a righteous man"* (2 Kings 4:1). By this we know that the Lord is bound to get involved. The widow only had a little bit of oil left in her home. Elijah commanded her to retrieve as many jars as she could find. When the widow did as the prophet had asked, God did an incredible miracle. The Lord began to fill every jar and vessel that the widow had collected. The Lord did not leave even one of her jars empty. God does not stay out of the affairs of the righteous; He will not let them down. He will never ignore their cries! Hebrews 11 is titled "heroes of the faith" and in this chapter there are many righteous people listed. In every story that is mentioned you will see God getting involved and stepping into action in the interest of a righteous person. Heaven partners with the righteous, God makes history with the righteous, and nothing can ever stand against them. Wherever you find a righteous person it is there where you will also find God. God walks beside those who are in right standing with Him, He acts on their behalf, and He always defends them! I want you to know that when you are righteous, there is no part of your life that you will have to face alone. When you are living righteously and set apart for God even what is meant to harm you becomes a blessing. Even when you stumble and fall God is waiting to use it to benefit you and never to wound you. In Romans 8:8 (NIV) it is promised that, *"all things God works for the good of those who love him."* When God gets involved in your story He turns the bad into good and the dark into light. When God gets involved He uses everything in your life to bless you! Throughout the Bible you will see God promoting and protecting the righteous; you will see God lifting them out of their troubles. Joseph was delivered and promoted by God many times throughout his life. David relied completely on the Lord for protection and victory in every battle and trial, and the Lord never failed him. God takes His righteous children from glory, to glory, to glory. As you study righteousness with me you will begin to understand that righteousness does not only grant you *one* thing. Righteousness is a package deal filled with many splendid blessings. When you walk in righteousness every one of these blessings now becomes your right.

**The Revelation of God's Word**

*"There are secret things that belong to the Lord our God, but the revealed things belong to us and we are descendants forever so that we may obey these wonderful words of the Lord."* This verse found in Deuteronomy 29:29 reveals something very vital to our study of righteousness. What remains secret belongs to God, but what is revealed to us is ours to keep. If you do not know the benefits of righteousness then you cannot enjoy them, but the moment that they are revealed to you they belong to you and all who are associated with you! As you study the word of God, the Holy Spirit will reveal truths and all that is revealed to you is a treasure that He has given to you.

  I was born to a very poor family. I remember once crying out to the Lord saying, "Lord, we cannot even afford a good meal. What must I do?" The Lord answered me and this was His reply: "Son, the best of creation is for the righteous. Open My Word and let me teach you about the benefits of righteousness." As the Lord revealed His gifts and benefits to me, I began to receive them. Money was supplied and prosperity began to flow into my life. No matter what I need or have needed, God has blessed me with it. The Lord has given me the funds and provision for everything He has

> **The Lord will never leave the righteous in their time of need.**

called me to do. I came to the realization that my emptiness is merely God's opportunity; if I am empty then it is only in order to be refilled! Fear no longer rules over any part of my life, because I am confident that the Lord will get involved in my every situation. The Lord will never leave the righteous in their time of need.

Since what remains hidden belongs to God and what is revealed belongs to us, it is crucial to meditate on His Word. It is one thing to know the scripture mentally, but it is another thing completely when it is revealed to you. A biblical concept or principle is important, but a revelation is something that cannot be taken away from you. In the Bible there is a man named Elisha who was a disciple and protégé of the prophet Elijah. Elisha spoke to Elijah in 2 Kings 2 and said, *"I want a double portion of your anointing."* To this Elijah replied, *"You have asked for a difficult thing, nevertheless if you see me being taken up by God, you can have what you ask."* Elijah is saying "if you see it then you can have it." One of the many miracles that Jesus did when He was on earth was open the eyes of the blind. If you study the book of 2 Corinthians it says, *"the god of the world has blinded their eyes so that they may not behold the Lord of glory."* If we do not behold Him then we cannot have Him. The devil intentionally attacks our sight and vision so that we may not behold the Lord of glory. Proverbs 29:18 (KJB) says, *"When there is no vision, the people perish."* If you ask the Lord to reveal Himself to you through His word, He is faithful to do so. I have never read the Bible simply because I enjoy reading stories. I read the Bible because as I read, I see the truth of God and everything that He reveals to me I can take hold of. Everything that He reveals to me is a gift that is mine to cherish forever!

## Identity In the Word of God

I would like you to understand how Jesus read scripture. In Luke 24:44 we find Jesus talking with His disciples. This incident in the Bible takes place after the resurrection of Christ. Jesus says to the disciples, *"When I was with you before, I told you that everything written about me by Moses and the prophets and in the Psalms must all come true."* In saying this, Jesus begins to reveal the truth of the scripture. All of the Old Testament books starting from Genesis to Malachi are a combination of major and minor Prophets, psalms, and the writings of Moses. Jesus said that all that had been written about Him in these books would be fulfilled. So, this means that throughout every book of the Old Testament we can see Jesus. This means that when Jesus would read the scripture He was not merely beholding random stories and beautiful songs. When Jesus was reading the scripture, He was beholding His very own identity written and hidden within every line! It is easy to assume that since Jesus was the Son of God He was born knowing His identity. We are actually told something contrary to this in Philippians 2 when it explains that Jesus was completely emptied of Himself when He came to earth. Jesus was not born with added advantages or privileges; God sent Jesus in the same way that He sent you and I. Jesus was in the womb for nine months and was born in a humble setting to humble parents. Jesus was not born knowing the scripture. Jesus had to learn how to invest His time into studying the Word of God and speaking with the Father. Jesus had to learn to let the Holy Spirit open His eyes to the scripture. In Luke 4:17(NIV) Jesus speaks something very interesting in the synagogue.

> *"And the scroll of the prophet Isaiah was handed to Him. Unrolling it, He found the place where it is written: 'The Spirit of the Lord is on me, because He has anointed me to proclaim good news to the poor. He has sent me to proclaim freedom for the prisoners and recovery of sight for the blind, to set the oppressed free, to proclaim the year of the Lord's favor.' Then he rolled up the scroll, gave it back to the attendant and sat down. The eyes of everyone in the synagogue were fastened on him. He began by saying to them, 'Today this scripture is fulfilled in your hearing.'"*

When Jesus read from the book of Isaiah He was not reading

the writings of a Prophet, Jesus was reading His own job description. Many people had read scripture in the synagogue, many of which had memorized it and knew it very well, but Jesus knew it was for Him. When Jesus read the scripture He let it manifest inside of Him because Jesus knew that it was written about Him! Throughout every book in the Old Testament Jesus found His identity, His job description, His belonging, and the Holy Spirit opened His eyes to see it. This is why when satan tempted and questioned Jesus, Jesus responded in a very specific way. Jesus did not say, "On the Jordan when I was baptized the heavens were opened and I was declared the beloved Son of God." Jesus did not use His personal experience to combat the attack of the enemy, instead Jesus replied saying, *"It is written."* This is why it is extremely important for us as children of God to understand the Bible and how to read it. When the devil promised Jesus many luxuries if He would only bow down, Jesus responded, *"You shall not tempt the LORD your God"* (Matthew 4:7 NKJV). Jesus saw His identity in the scripture and when this happened the enemy lost all power!

I want you to capture this one truth: the books of the Bible are *for* us but they can only *benefit* us if they are revealed *to* us. If you do not read the Bible from a place of revelation then, my friend, you are reading someone else's story. When you read the Bible your perspective is very important. You cannot read the Bible as a storybook filled with other people's experiences, but rather, you must begin to see yourself within the scriptures! When you begin to read and understand the Bible in this way, you will also begin to efficiently defend against the enemy. You will see victory in your everyday life. You will no longer be searching for God's will, but you will begin walking out the will in which He has already revealed to you through His word. You will begin walking in the same authority that Jesus walked in. It is very important that you learn who you are; that you find your identity in the Word. When satan attempted to discourage and attack Jesus all that Jesus had to do was speak out His identity. Jesus knew exactly where His identity was found in the Bible and because of this the devil fled from Him immediately. When you know your identity the enemy will flee, the enemy cannot attach to you. If you go back to the very beginning of time you will find that a lack of identity has been an ongoing issue. When Eve was in the garden the serpent convinced her that if she ate the forbidden fruit she would become like God. If only Eve had known her identity, she would have understood that she was already like God; made in His very image. The devil can only fool those who do not know their identity, and your identity must be found in the word of God.

When Jesus walked the earth He did not become familiar with the word of God in one day or at one moment. Jesus read and studied the word day by day, diligently learning and seeking the Father's voice. Isaiah 50:4 (NKJV) says,

> *"The Lord God has given me the tongue of the learned, that I should know how to speak a word in season to Him who is weary. He awakens me morning by morning, He awakens my ear to hear as the learned. The Lord God has opened my ear; and I was not rebellious, nor did I turn away. I gave my back to those who struck me, and my cheeks to those who plucked out the beard; I did not hide my face from shame and spitting."*

This Messianic prophecy is speaking of our Lord and savior, Jesus Christ. This scripture is explaining that the Father taught Jesus daily, *morning by morning*. Jesus did not do it on His own. Jesus let the Holy Spirit teach Him. Jesus chose every day to seek the Father and do His will. One interesting part of this scripture is when it says, *"I was not rebellious, nor did I turn away. I gave my back to those who struck me, and my cheeks to those who plucked out the beard; I did not hide my face from shame and spitting."* Jesus did not fight back against His oppressors when He was being crucified because of one reason. Jesus was awoken morning by morning by God, who taught Him, and directed His steps. When Jesus was awoken on the morning of His crucifixion the Father told Him to submit to the beatings, the suffering, and the pain of the cross. When

Jesus heard the Father's will He did not rebel, but He submitted and offered Himself to His persecutors. Jesus embraced every part of His identity and He did not let anyone mislead Him from the path in which God had placed at His feet. When Peter had heard that Jesus was to be crucified he responded saying, *"Far be it from You, Lord; this shall not happen to You!"* (Matthew 16:22 NKJV). But Jesus corrected Him and spoke out in the next verse, *"Get behind Me, Satan! You are an offense to Me, for you are not mindful of the things of God, but the things of men."* Isn't it interesting how Jesus and His disciples were on the same team and yet, they both viewed what was about to take place in very different ways? When something is revealed to you it will change the way that you approach it. Peter regarded the crucifixion with a terrible mistake, while Jesus embraced this assignment as the will of God.

Jesus learned the Father's voice and studied the Father's word daily, and Jesus did this privately before He ever did it publicly. You must understand that you can only do in public what the Lord has taught you to do in private. Jesus set this example for us. He did not begin doing miracles and walking in confident power in one moment. Jesus sought the Father and grew in faith and knowledge in the secret place before He went into any public settings.

It is often written that Jesus would go into the wilderness to pray. Luke 22:39 says that it was His *custom* to spend all night in prayer. A custom is something that is done specifically and regularly, and this is how Jesus devoted His time to the Father. You are given the same tools that Jesus possessed, the same Spirit, the same Father, the same power. Everyday it is up to you what you will do with the tools you have been given and where you will devote your time. Every day you must read the word of God from a place of fresh revelation and you must ask the Lord to reveal His word to you. Jesus promised us that the Spirit of truth would come and lead us. When you need understanding, when you need revelation, let the Holy Spirit be the one to guide you. In Luke 24:45 (NKJV) Jesus opens the minds of the disciples so that they would begin to grasp His words and the words of the Father. *"And He opened their understanding, that they might comprehend the scriptures."* In doing this, Jesus opened their eyes and the scripture began to come alive to them. My friend, God has the power to open your eyes to His word so that you would begin to see your identity within each verse. Jesus' identity was found and formed in the scriptures and so it must be with *every* believer.

> God involves Himself in every part of a righteous person's life. He personally teaches them and reveals to them His will.

God involves Himself in every part of a righteous person's life. He personally teaches them and reveals to them His will.

As you begin to find your identity in the word of God you will also find confidence in the promises of the Lord. What God reveals to you is yours to keep; the treasure that you uncover within His word belongs to you. When your eyes are opened to the blessings of righteousness and the true identity that has been given to you by God, nothing will be able to stop you! Even that which is formed against you will be turned from evil to good. I want you to know that the righteous cannot be defeated. Psalms 125:3 (TPT) tells us that, *"The wicked will not always rule over the godly, provoking them to do what is evil."* This means that the righteous are still prone to mistakes, but this does not make them wicked. You are righteous because God declares you righteous, not because of what you have to offer. The righteous may be *provoked to do what is evil*, this may be because of temptation or lack of submission to God. The righteous may stumble and fall, but even when a righteous man falls down seven times he will always get back up! The righteous cannot be defeated! If your circumstances tell you that you are a slave, watch the Lord raise you up into royalty like He did with Joseph. Or if you feel trapped in a den of lions, watch the Lord silence their mouths before you and grant you favor in every place that you step like He did for Daniel. If the world around you is rotten and filled to the brim with evil, watch the Lord wash it like a flood and lift you above the waves like He did for Noah.

Remember that your identity is found in the Word of God. Jesus was a good student and He always listened to the Father; He only did what He saw the Father doing. Each of us as children of God must become good students and good listeners. We must practice every day to hear and obey the voice of God. We must read the Bible from a place of revelation and take every step from a place of confidence in what God has spoken! When we do this we will go from glory to glory to glory, never living any part of our lives in a place of lack. The blessings in store for each of us are beyond what we can imagine. *Morning by morning* we must come to the Lord in secret and soon His power will manifest, influence, and be known publicly!

# Chapter 11

# **Righteousness and Works**

When the Church of Christ was born it began moving and growing at a rapid pace. Churches began sprouting up in many different regions and cultures and because of this there stemmed a problem. Skewed theologies and mixed beliefs began to infiltrate the church. Even men and women from Jerusalem would join the nearest churches and pollute the gospel of Jesus by adding unnecessary ideals and rules. This is why Paul spoke a great deal of grace and the foundational truths of Christianity in the book of Colossians. This context is vital as we begin to examine the words of James.

*"You see that a person is justified by works and not by faith alone"* (James 2:24 ESV). By writing this James is correcting the attitude of the people and saying something incredibly important. . James is not saying that we must work in order to become righteous. James is explaining that when we are made righteous *by* God we are in turn made able to walk righteously *with* Him! In the same chapter James also says, *"Thus also faith by itself, if it does not have works, is dead"* (James 2:17 NKJV). The most indispensable element that you must gather from this verse is what James is saying about faith. You can work without faith, but you cannot have faith without it producing the true works of God as a result. Jesus revealed a beautiful truth for us when He spoke the words, *"I am the vine; you are the branches. Whoever abides in me and I in him, he it is that bears much fruit, for apart from me you can do nothing"* (John 15:5 ESV). Whatever you do should produce fruit; it should become visible to those around you. A woman who is pregnant should not always have the need to explain that she is pregnant, for day by day her pregnancy will become more and more visible - so it should be with our fruit! Many problems stem from the fact that our flesh desires fruit without the willingness to first put down roots. When we begin to grasp the concept that certain roots

produce certain fruits, then there will be much breakthrough within us.

The early church was struggling to understand the concept of roots and fruits and because of this, division began to seep in. Some would read the scripture and garner a belief system, while another would read and construct an opposing one! *"Some will say, 'you have faith and I have works'"* (James 2:14 NKJV). This verse alone reveals the empty quarrels that had been tearing the church apart. James at this time was the leader of the church and he addresses this issue by responding in the same verse, *"Show me your faith apart from your works, and I'll show you my faith by my works."* James is insisting that our faith is not truly faith unless it alters the way we act, the way we speak, and the way we think! Nothing within you will stay within you. It will overflow and pour out of you, it will be seen in your eyes, heard on your lips, and felt in your presence. James never said that our works are what dictate our salvation, rather James is explaining the fruit in which our union with Christ is meant to bear. You must understand that the Lord has deleted *"works"* from the root and has instead rewritten them as the fruit. The root has now become Christ and in Him all good works will grow. This is why the scripture tells us that we are created in Christ for *good works*! If a thief meets Jesus and gives his life to the Lord, the *fruits*, or, *works* that are to follow will be seen in his behavior. The thief will refrain from stealing and instead, he will become generous and selfless as he walks with Christ. In Ephesians 4:24 (NKJV), Apostle Paul urged the Church saying, *"And that you put on the new man which was created according to God, in true righteousness and holiness."* He goes on to instruct in verse 28, *"Let him who stole steal no longer, but rather let him labor, working with his hands what is good, that he may have something to give him who has need."*

James is saying that faith cannot stand on its own, that when we believe we must take a step. Belief without action is not belief at all. In James 2:19 (NKJV) James tells us another important truth by saying, *"You believe that there is one God. You do well. Even the demons believe—and tremble! But do you want to know, O foolish man, that faith without works is dead?"* My friend, faith must produce good works and it cannot be the other way around.

Paul writes to the early church in the book of Galatians addressing something extremely pertinent because once again, the Church was in crisis. Hellenistic Jews had invaded the church and began convincing the new Christians that it was by the law of Moses that we are saved. The Galatians were being lied to; these Jewish leaders were swindling them. When Paul saw that these born again, spirit filled believers of Christ were turning back to the law he addressed them saying, *"O foolish Galatians! Who has bewitched you...?" (Galatians 3:1 NKJV).* The problem was that they were forsaking Christ and going back to dead works. There is something mentioned in the following verses that is important to note. Paul refers to their works as *"Dead works, the works of flesh."* In this we perceive that there are two different kinds of works: *good works* and *dead works*. The difference between these two almost identical actions is, quite simply, the order in which they are placed. In the book of Galatians, Paul explains to us what dead works really are. If you are depending on your works in order to receive salvation and gain favor with God then you are living from death and dead works. When your works become the root, my friend, it is death. It is death because it is the motion of forsaking the Law of freedom in Christ and turning back to the law of sin and death. In James we see the beauty and truth about good works and what and where God intended them to be. Good works must stem from the life union in which you have with God. Good works are purely the result of Christ living within you. Jesus is our great example, our perfect role model, and He never acted out of fear or obligation. Jesus was first privately anointed, accepted, and loved by the Father, and then He was released to do good works. Jesus simply watched the Father and did what He saw and it was from this place, from this root, that good works sprung up like a carefully tended garden!

In the days in which James was living, he was encountering some extremely apathetic people. He was encountering people who did not desire to change their ways and people who used faith as a crutch in order to live selfishly. James is saying that if you have faith then fruits will grow; fruits of patience, love, forgiveness, and sacrifice. James is saying that if your faith does not touch the rest of your life then there is a problem. Since Jesus lives inside of you, your life must begin to resemble Jesus more and more everyday. Since your spirit has become one with the Father, you must learn to walk in His footsteps.

In learning this you will begin to see certain pieces of the Bible clearer. For example, if you continue reading in James there is something controversial that is written. *"Was not our father Abraham justified by works as he offered Isaac his son on the altar"* (James 2:21 NKJV)? I have heard people say that such a statement is contrary to what Paul says in Romans four. Paul makes a similar, yet very different claim when he says, *"Was not Abraham our father justified by faith in Christ Jesus?"* James speaks of works while Paul is speaking of faith, but so much is lost in hasty assumptions. When you look closely at these statements, you will notice that they are presenting two very different outcomes, from two very different ingredients. Paul speaks about justification and righteousness through faith - "it was by faith that Abraham was justified." James speaks of something different. After the justification and the acceptance, after God had declared Abraham righteous, because of his faith, fruits began to bloom. Abraham's faith was confirmed by his works; his works sealed in action what was done in belief! James then writes, *"And by works faith is made perfect"* (James 2:22 NKJV). When you study the book of James you will begin to understand that he is building off of what Paul has written to the church and in turn he is confirming it. Paul says that you are justified and found righteous by faith and James builds on that saying, let your faith be confirmed by your works; let your faith bear fruit!

## The Law in Question

Jesus said that it is foolish to put old wine into new wineskins and new wine into old wineskins because they would destroy each other. Similarly, mixing Covenants will have this same effect. It will rupture the beauty that God has created. Grace and the law do not fuse. Many have stumbled when attempting to blend what was never intended to touch. There are things in the Old and New Covenants that seem at first to contradict; however, there is something extraordinary about the law. Every question regarding the law will, if asked in the right context, only point you to Jesus himself.

> Every question regarding the law will, if asked in the right context, only point you to Jesus himself.

It is once again extremely important to understand the circumstance and context of every story in the Bible. James is the leader of a newborn church; an infant church. James and Paul have a difficult job as they are called to teach a new way to those who have known and practiced one way all of their lives. These courageous heroes of the faith were missionaries in a place in which the first persecutors of Christians arose. Jesus, His teachings, and His followers suddenly began questioning a law that had been chosen and embraced for ages. As a result, different philosophies began to emerge throughout the surrounding regions. Contradicting beliefs began to confuse and stir up division among the young church. With so many new believers and different convictions, a culture of accusation and gossip began to arise. Such a culture is contrary to God's will and body. Finally one of the greatest and most fragile aspects of the church was shattered - its unity! It is crucial that you understand the position in which James finds himself. James was the leader of the congregation at this time and he addresses the issue in his letter to the church. In James 4:11-12 (NKJV), he appeals to the church saying,

> *"Do not speak evil of one another, brethren. He who speaks evil of a brother and judges his brother, speaks evil of the law and judges the law. But if you judge the law, you are not a doer of the law but a judge. There is*

> *one Lawgiver, who is able to save and to destroy. Who are you to judge another?"*

I would like you to understand this in the context of a family. If a mother comes home to find her kids bickering and acting aggressively towards one another, she might tell the kids to go to their rooms and sit quietly. The mother commands them to do this because a time of quiet reflection is important before moving any further in resolving this conflict. If the kids, however, were to take this out of context they might garner an idea that their mother has commanded them never to speak. The kids might begin to believe that their mother does not like to hear their opinions or consider their words. This conclusion would be absurd because the context clearly shows the reasoning for her command. Context is vital to every part of our life. I hope you can see that when James is commanding the church to follow the law, he is not referring to their old religious ways, but to the new law! In Matthew 22:40 Jesus said that the two greatest laws are these, to love your God and love each other. Jesus said that every other law given by the prophets hangs on these two. Some theologians have claimed that James is speaking of the law of Moses. There is no place within the law of Moses, however, in which we are given any guidance or commands that address speaking against a brother. The new law gives us direct guidance saying, *"A new commandment I give to you, that you love one another: just as I have loved you, you also are to love one another"* (John 13:34 ESV). These are the words of Jesus. James is saying that they are living contrary to the law of Christ and he is reminding the church to love as Christ has loved.

It is also crucial to understand the different uses of the word "law." Some have muddled their own thinking by a simple error of words. There is something distinct written in Proverbs 28:4 (NLT), *"To reject the law is to praise the wicked; to obey the law is to fight them."* You must understand that God was using the law to guide His people during this time. The law was necessary only to point to our true salvation. When Jesus came, He fulfilled and dissolved the law creating a new and life-giving law to all who will believe. In Solomon's day and age, however, the law was all God had given and He was using it to modify and change their behavior. I would also like you to understand that Solomon was a king. He ruled over his country and like any ruler, there was a law that had been instituted. In every nation there are traffic laws, tax laws, and criminal laws. Laws govern the public. If rules are not implemented then the culture and society will be prone to chaos and disorder. Solomon as a king is addressing his nation saying that disregarding rules and authority is walking in wickedness. It is important to be watchful and decipher between when the word is speaking of the Mosaic Law and when it is addressing a governing law. Solomon reminds his people that although they are a chosen generation and precious in the sight of the Lord, they must also live as righteous citizens of their earthly home. There is a spiritual side as well as a physical, and the Lord sees both. He works in both, and both will be accounted for.

There is another question regarding the law. This question stems from a passage found in the book of Ezekiel. Ezekiel 43:12 (ESV) reads, *"This is the law of the temple: the whole territory on the top of the mountain all around shall be most holy. Behold, this is the law of the temple."* In the Old Testament we see how God is able to sanctify certain locations. From Genesis until Malachi you will find people building shrines and altars where individuals from all over the nation would come to offer sacrifices. The prophet Ezekiel is proclaiming that the location in which the temple is placed is holy. The temple itself is not what makes this place holy, it is the presence of God that makes it holy. God dwells in His temple and that is what sets it apart; that is what sanctifies the land around it. When Moses was met by the burning bush, the voice of the Lord spoke out to him. This voice told Moses that he was walking on holy ground. The ground itself was not inherently holy, it was no different from the ground that dwelt a mile away. What then made this ground holy? The answer is this: the Holy One came down! The presence of God is what hallowed that soil and sanctified that dirt. Jesus Himself said in Matthew 23:17, *"Oh foolish people, tell me one thing, is it the gold that sanctifies the altar or is it the altar that sanctifies the gold which is sacrificed on, which is greater?"* The temple was not holy on its own accord, but it was holy due to the fact that the presence of the Holy One dwelt there.

We are in a different time, a time in which God no longer has to sanctify places and things, because He sanctifies people! The old way could not be sustained; the old way could not bring true freedom. The Old Covenant was a broken system. You see, a habitual liar, robber, or adulterer, would come to the temple and put on an attire of holiness, but on the inside they remained in chains. So many would perform while at the altar, but the moment that they left, they would resort back to their wickedness. This is why the Lord said that He would rewrite the law in our minds. The Lord has made us holy from the inside out. This is incredible news! The sacrifice of Jesus Christ has made a way to make *people* holy. Now as we walk in this dark and sinful world, we do not have to be overcome by it. In the days before Jesus, walking in sanctity and holiness was seasonal, but we are no longer in those days. We are in the days that Jesus spoke of when He said in John 4:14, *"The water that I give you will become within you, streams of living water."* Jesus demolished the confinement of the temple in three days and then He rebuilt it within *you,* just as He had promised to do. Your holiness is no longer based on placement or geography, but on the One who lives within you! You have become the temple of the Lord; you are now where He dwells. The moment that you invited the Lord inside of you, He transformed you into the light,the light of the world. I hope you understand that the Bible never contradicts itself, and every question that you have will lead you deeper and closer to the Lord. Every question regarding the law should only point to Jesus and the New Covenant, for that is what God intended it to do.

## The Righteous are Set Apart!

There are a great many things that a righteous person is called to do. The Lord has extraordinary plans for the righteous! One of the calls of the righteous is to walk in the world but not be consumed by it. Psalms 1:1(NLT) states, *"Oh, the joys of those who do not follow the advice of the wicked, or stand around with sinners, or join in with scoffers."* Now, if we flip to the New Testament, the book of Matthew tells us something interesting about Jesus. In Matthew 9:10 we are told that many tax collectors and sinners gathered and reclined with Jesus. Jesus was known as a friend to the prostitutes and sinners, and the Pharisees considered this a great abomination. The verse in psalms, however, is referring to those who take counsel from the wicked; it is speaking of those who walk a slippery path. Jesus walked among sinners, but He did not walk in their ways. When Jesus spoke of the disciples to the Father, He asked that they not be taken out *of* the world, but rather, that they would be preserved while they walked *in* the world. Paul wrote saying that we are to be *in* this world, and yet, we are not to be *of* it. As Christians we are not called to be an isolated group of people, we are called to love the world like the Father does. Paul said that for the Jewish he became a Jew, for the Gentiles he became a Gentile, and for the Greeks he became a Greek. Paul did not do this in order to manipulate, but in order to reach and save the lost. A problem only occurs when you begin to let the ungodly influence infect and guide you. We are told in Romans 12:21 (ESV) to, *"Overcome evil with good."* Jesus walked out this example in each situation that was presented to Him. He used it as an opportunity to love and save all who were in reach. Romans 12:1-2 reminds us, *"Do not be conformed to the ways of the world, but by the renewing of your mind may your life change, that you may know the perfect and acceptable will of God."* The first call of the righteous is to be in this world, but not of it; it is to be a light in a very vast darkness.

**The Righteous are Generous!**

Another call of the righteous is generosity. You cannot be righteous and simultaneously stingy; these attributes do not blend. As you walk righteously the Lord will take away your heart of greed and hand you a heart of benevolence and generosity. In Luke 6 (NLT) it says,

> *"Give to anyone who asks; and when things are taken away from you, don't try to get them back. Do to others as you would like them to do to you. If you love only those who love you, why should you get credit for that? Even sinners love those who love them! And if you do good only to those who do good to you, why should you get credit? Even sinners do that much! And if you lend money only to those who can repay you, why should you get credit? Even sinners will lend to other sinners for a full return. Love your enemies! Do good to them. Lend to them without expecting to be repaid. Then your reward from heaven will be very great, and you will truly be acting as children of the Most High, for he is kind to those who are unthankful and wicked."*

These words that Jesus had spoken to the Jewish people were extremely radical at the time. Jesus was asking something of them in which they could not do in their own strength. Now, we know and have carefully analyzed over the course of this book that our Sonship is not based on works. Our Sonship as Christians is based solely and completely on Jesus and our belief in Him. 1 John 3:1 (NKJV) tells us, "Behold what manner of love the Father has bestowed on us, that we should be called children of God!" It was love that made a way for us to be sons and daughters, not our own efforts and attempts. In the scripture passage from Luke, however, Jesus says *if* you are generous and love those who cannot love you back, then your reward will be great. He says that then, you will be children of the Most High. Jesus is doing something very specific in saying this: He is breaking new ground and opening their minds. Since what Jesus is asking of them is so extreme and seemingly impossible, He is actually pointing them to salvation. When Jesus calls you to do what is impossible with man, what He is really saying is, "let me do it through you." Jesus through these verses is telling the crowd that unless you are born again you cannot be righteous. Unless you are born again you cannot be a Son of God, you cannot be truly generous or loving. The only way that we can walk in the characteristics of Jesus is to let Him live inside of us and to give Him control. This is the truth about generosity: it is a gift and fruit of righteousness. Generosity is a quality that is a struggle for most, but for those who walk in righteousness it is simply their primary nature. Proverbs 37:21 (ESV) states clearly, "The wicked borrows but does not pay back, but the righteous is generous and gives." " To the righteous, generosity is a part of their DNA because they do not rely on money, but on Jesus. To the righteous, generosity is not a struggle or a burden because provision is plentiful in the kingdom of God. There is no lack for the righteous and they are established; their heart is anchored deeply in the Lord!

## The Righteous are Caring!

There are many callings on the life of a righteous person, one of them being the call to be caring. Proverbs 29:7 (NIV) says that *"The righteous care about justice for the poor."* Proverbs 12:10 (NIV) goes even a step further to say that, *"The righteous care for the needs of their animals."* The righteous are called to delight themselves in the Lord and in His word. The righteous are called to rise above their trials and obstacles; they are to be established and grounded. The righteous are to be fearless and courageous, they are as bold as lions and they cannot be overcome. None of this, however, can be done in their own strength; none of this can be attained through vain works. The Lord is calling us first to come to Him and receive all He desires to give us. The righteous ones of God, throughout history, have accomplished supernatural and unforgettable successes. They have marked and changed our world drastically throughout all ages, but it would be foolish to assume that they did any of it on their own. We do nothing on our own. Isaiah 64:6 tells us that we cannot attain righteousness on our own. Nothing we have is complete, rather it has been broken and corrupted by sin and the fall of creation. In Romans 4:18, Paul explains to us that our fallen and fleshly nature stands in opposition to the righteousness of God. He must increase as our selfish and fickle nature decreases. The Lord has not called you into a life of striving and misery, but into a life of freedom and prosperity!

We are told in Proverbs 4:18 (ESV) that, *"The path of the righteous is like the light of dawn, which shines brighter and brighter until full day."* The path and call of righteousness is significant and extreme; it is immense and filled to the brim with awe! But, my friend, you will never once have to walk it alone. You will never be left empty, broken, or forsaken, and He will be with you to the end of the age.

## Chapter 12

# Righteousness and the Truth of Who You Are

There were two challenges that Paul began to face within the church of Galatia. The first issue stemmed from those who did not understand the concept of grace. A misconception of grace resulted in a susceptibility to lawlessness and immoral conduct. The second problem was with those who did not understand the concept of *salvation*. Those who did not understand salvation became prone to legalism and the bondage of religion. We see here that Paul is faced with a difficult situation, but something very beautiful stems from this. When Paul begins to see the darkness and confusion that is growing within the church, he gives a very clear and important message to the people.

### The Kingdom of God

> *"When you follow the desires of your sinful nature, the results are very clear: sexual immorality, impurity, lustful pleasures, idolatry, sorcery, hostility, quarreling, jealousy, outbursts of anger, selfish ambition, dissension, division, envy, drunkenness, wild parties, and other sins like these. Let me tell you again, as I have before, that anyone living that sort of life will not inherit the Kingdom of God." (Galatians 5:19-21 NLT)*

Paul reframes and refocuses the subject matter from salvation and grace to *"the kingdom of God."* He is asking a simple question, *"What are you following?"*

It is important that you learn and remember something extraordinarily crucial about the Kingdom of God. You must learn what it is to abide. Although you are saved and born again through grace, the choice to abide still remains. Jesus tells us that the branch that abides in Him will bear much fruit! Through the cross and your belief in Christ you have inherited a sonship that cannot be ripped away. You must not take advantage of this gift, however, and in turn reject the lordship of God. If you study the parable of the prodigal son it will become clear to you that the path in which the son took did not lose him his sonship. When the prodigal son lived in rebellion he lost and squandered his inheritance, not his sonship. You will always remain a child of God even if you are a disobedient one. This is what Paul was making unmistakably clear to the Galatians. Paul was imploring them to put away their fears and pretenses regarding salvation and grace, and to look up to the great inheritance of the Kingdom of God! If you cling to anything outside of Christ you will begin to lose the Kingdom of God, for the Kingdom itself is the person of Christ! Everything finds its meaning and purpose together in Christ, so whether it is legalism or lawlessness, it will draw you astray from your ultimate design and identity.

Paul does not stop at the sin in which we are to avoid, but in Galatians 5:22-23 (NLT) he goes on to assure us of a righteous path radiant with the holiness of God. *"The Holy Spirit produces this kind of fruit in our lives: love, joy, peace, patience, kindness, goodness, faithfulness, gentleness, and self-control."* Paul is presenting us with two paths that a born-again believer is offered. One path is to receive salvation yet continue to live in bondage and forsake the inheritance. The other path is to be renewed; to be transformed and receive everything that the Lord has in store! The Lord has so many incredible things planned for each one of us and all of them are irrevocable. But when you live a compromised life your path will become fruitless and futile. If you were given a knife, you would quickly find that what could be accomplished with this weapon would be limited based on its sharpness. The same goes for all of the gifts awaiting you.

If you live in a state of dullness you will be restricted and stunted. Understanding the Kingdom of God begins when you understand that abiding in the Lord is a choice; beholding the Lord is a decision. Paul digs up the root of each of the problems presented to him and reveals to us that what we follow and what we see is where we go and who we become. Almost every problem that we face today is directly tied to a lack of identity and a brokenness in our image. The enemy always attacks our sight because it is what we behold that, in turn, we become.

> Almost every problem that we face today is directly tied to a lack of identity and a brokenness in our image

**God's Eyes**

You will often see yourself from the lens of how you feel: from your emotions, your preferences, the opinions of others, and so on. I believe that there are three mirrors which exist within our world. The first, and the most commonly known, is the physical mirror. The physical mirror reflects a physical reflection of who you are on the outside. A physical mirror will show you both the faults and beauties found in your appearance. It will reflect every imperfection and insecurity that you may try to hide. Then there is an emotional mirror. This mirror is based on what people think and say about you. When the world looks at you and tells you who you are, that is your emotional mirror. Our emotions are determined by how people treat and address us; they change with every word and action of those around us. Just as a physical mirror may reveal to us our physical faults, so an emotional mirror will reveal the faults in our inner-lives. Looking into an emotional mirror can be tiring to our souls. There is one more mirror, and this mirror will not wear down our spirits. The last mirror is the word of God. The word of God reveals to us what is in our spirit, soul, and ultimately our entire being! Of the three, it is the only mirror that is eternal; it is permanent, and always rooted in love. God does not hate His children. He does not hate sinners, He does not even hate those who tortured and murdered his son. God is not cruel, He is gentle and forgiving, Luke 6:35 (NLT) says that, *"He is kind to those who are unthankful and wicked."* In this we know that our Father is good, He is gracious, and the lens in which He sees His children is very different from the lens in which they see themselves.

The answer to the question, *"how does God see me?"* is so important. Some wonder if He sees us like the angels, or the demons, or as just another piece of creation. How do you believe God sees you? Do you believe that He is emotionally attached to you; that your life and happiness matters to Him? The truth of it all lies in what I think you may already know. God found you when you were covered in your sin, He paid the greatest price for you when you felt worthless. He sought you when you did not seek Him. He interceded for you when you were yet His enemy. He chose you when you were abandoned, loved you when you were broken.

> *"For it was always in His perfect plan to adopt us as His delightful children, through our union with Jesus, the anointed one, so that His tremendous love that cascades over us would glorify His grace, for the same love He has for the beloved Jesus, He has for us. And this unfolding plan brings Him great pleasure!"* (Ephesians 1:5-6 TPT)

This verse reveals the truth about how God sees you. Beloved Child of the Most High, He created you for Himself. Out of all of His creation, nothing delights our God more than us, His very own. God spoke the words *"it is good"* after creating every piece of creation except for man. When God created man He marveled and said, *"It is very good."* There is endless angelic worship that is lavished on our King and yet, we are told that God leaves heaven to come and dwell with us, that God delights in the praises of His people. We are told that He builds His throne upon our worship and in this we know that God has created us for Himself. Jesus said that He has come to seek and save the lost. My friend, you cannot lose something that did not originally

> **When you change the way you see God it will change the way you see yourself!**

belong to you. If you are lost, it is only proof that you belong to Him! If you are wandering, or broken, or dissatisfied with this world, it is in fact evidence of your belonging to the Father and your birthright in heaven! You have been created by God *for* God and nothing can comfort the heart of God like you can. The Lord has created you for Himself and He is jealous for you. He has given everything in His power to draw you back and to find you when you were adrift. The price that was paid for you has put value on your life like nothing else could have. God has said that you are worth dying for and in doing so has lifted you above all creation. The Lord has called you family; you are no longer a stranger to God but a child in His arms. Hebrews 2:11 (NLT) states, *"So now Jesus and the ones he makes holy have the same Father. That is why Jesus is not ashamed to call them his brothers and sisters."* How beautiful is the revelation that Jesus is not ashamed of you! So often we let our skewed perception of God dictate how we see ourselves. If we believe that Jesus is ashamed of us we may begin to distance ourselves from Him. This is why Adam hid himself in the garden. His sin had fragmented his view of God and he felt shame for the first time. God, however, was not angry. God's heart was broken and He desired to find Adam to restore him, but when God came looking for him, Adam was hiding. When you change the way you see God it will change the way you see yourself! When you see what the Father has done for you and what Jesus feels about you, you can no longer say that you are an orphan. The orphan spirit afflicts the children of God, but the moment that it is broken off of you the fear of living life alone will also break off! The fear of being left behind will disappear and the fear of being unprotected will be no more! There is an assurance and a confidence, a courage and a fearlessness, that comes to the one who knows that they belong.

My son knew a young man who had no family and when this young man would find himself in trouble, my son would ask me to send money to help his friend. I believe that this is a beautiful picture of how our relationship and sonship with the Lord can affect and influence those around us. When my son would ask, I would always give him what he needed so that he could support his friend who didn't have a father. The heavenly Father does the same for us. When the orphan spirit is broken off of you and when you know who you are and who your Father is, the blessings in your life will overflow into everyone around you! As a child of God you have all the authority and every right that Jesus had. There are no grandchildren in the kingdom of God. The very moment that I was born again I became a son of God and the very moment that my son was born again he also became a son of God. Every single one of us are given the same opportunities and the same inheritance that Jesus Christ was! It all starts from the moment that we see ourselves through the eyes of God.

I want to break off a major misconception that many believers have let skew their vision of God. Your past is a major part of who you are; it is a part of your testimony. Oftentimes, however, people let their past become their identity and this is extremely detrimental. You must understand that the lens in which God sees you is not filtered through your past and what you've done. When God sees you, He sees a new creation. He sees a piece of His very heart, an image of Himself, born again and completely fresh. This is why Jesus told Nicodemus, *"unless one is born again, he cannot see the kingdom of God"* (John 3:33 NKJV). Once you enter into the kingdom of God you become a new creation. Old things are past and everything becomes new. You are not a modified creation, or a rejuvenated one, you are a new creation and you are no longer defined by your past. The enemy has nothing to use against us anymore. God does not recognize you by your past; He sees you as something that has never existed until now! You are remade before His eyes.

## God In You

One of the greatest accomplishments of the cross that is often looked over is our redemption. In the last chapter I broke down what it means to be the temple of God, and I would like to dive into this idea a bit further.

God no longer sanctifies temples and locations, but He now sanctifies people! As God created a body for Jesus and He himself was led by the Spirit, God did it again and called it "a new creation." You now have the Spirit of the living God dwelling inside of you. The spirit that healed the sick, saved the lost, and raised the dead is now present beneath your very skin. You are no longer an easy target for the enemy. Adam, the first man to walk the earth, dwelt with God, but you and I have become one with God!

> Adam, the first man to walk the earth, dwelt with God, but you and I have become one with God!

The new creation is far superior than anything that the Old Covenant has seen. The Spirit would fall on Samson and he would do mighty things, but when the Spirit would leave him, he would be left an ordinary man. My friend, now when God comes inside of a person something changes; something happens that has never happened before. When Peter walked the streets after the Spirit had entered into him, many witnessed the healing of those to whom even his shadow touched. The shadow that fell on the ground was no longer the shadow of Peter, but the shadow of the living God. Every limit that you put upon yourself will be broken the moment that you begin to see the truth and walk in it! If there is lack, turn the water into wine. If there is sickness, cleanse it. If there is bondage, break the chains. If there is death, say "Lazarus come forth." For the things that are impossible with man are possible with God!

You are the light of the world and I implore you not to limit your world. There is no more time to waste by seeing your *world* as a small sphere. Paul tells us in Ephesians 3:10 (ESV) that, *"through the church the manifold wisdom of God might now be made known to the rulers and authorities in the heavenly realms."* The light within you reaches the heavens, it fills this world and spills over into every part of creation. God does not put a maximum limit on anyone's gifting or calling. All you have been given is enough to change and alter the world and every person within it. It is you who defines how far you will go and how much you will do. God is ready; He is waiting to do through you something infinitely more than you could ask or imagine!

Just a glimpse through the eyes of the Lord, just a peek at how He sees you will alter your life forever. Imagine living the rest of your life with His vision; imagine everyday from here on out walking in the identity that God has cultivated for you since the beginning of time. Every step that you take toward seeing yourself through His eyes is a step you take toward sincere freedom and abundant life! Your Father speaks the truth over your identity. When you hear Him say that you are valuable, you begin to feel valued. When your father says that you are His and only His, that you are no longer a stranger or a foreigner, you begin to feel a confidence and boldness knowing that you now belong. When your Father tells you that you are free and guiltless, redeemed and made completely new, your shame will disappear. When you see your Father smiling at you, your fears will perish and your heart will heal. You are complete and cherished before His eyes. God finds no fault in you and according to Zephaniah 3:17, your Father rejoices over you with loud singing! We have a God and a Father who cannot love in part. He loves in whole, fully and completely!

Since the beginning of time the enemy has tried to convince the children of God that they lacked what they needed. Though Adam and Eve were given all that they could have asked for, Satan pointed out what they didn't have. Jesus Christ never lived in lack. When the disciples brought five loaves and two fish they told Jesus that there was not enough. The disciples were focused on what they lacked. Jesus thanked the Father, broke the bread, and fed over five thousand people! Jesus did not see what He lacked, He saw what God had given to Him. Your Father does not speak of what you lack, He speaks of who you are and what you have in Him! Look at the victory awaiting. "Be wise as to what is good and innocent as to what is evil. The God of peace will soon crush Satan under your feet" (Romans

16:20-21 ESV). This truth proves that Satan no longer has the authority to speak into your life or influence your identity. Your Father says that He will crush Satan under your feet. You carry the glory of God, you are the bride of Christ, and you are seated in heavenly places ruling and reigning with the Lord. This is who you are, this is who your Father sees you as, and this is the mirror that is eternal! Hallelujah!

I invite you wherever you are, to look into the mirror. Look deep and hard and take in everything you see. My friend, look into the mirror of His word because that is where you will discover the truth of who you are; that is where you will look through the eyes of your Father, and you will never see yourself the same again!

## Chapter 13

# Righteousness & The blood

Let me show you something. I want to talk about the Blood Covenant. When Jesus said, 'This is my new covenant in my blood,' what did He refer to? Many of us think He was referring to the covenant that God cut in Genesis 15 with Abraham. You know that time Abraham was not called Abraham; he was just Abram. He was a gentile, and, amazingly, he was not even circumcised, yet God cut a covenant for him. Do you realize that God does not wait for you to change and then make a covenant, but God makes a covenant first and then changes you? Abram, you will become Abraham, and Sarai, you will become Sarah. Why? Because of the covenant I am in with you. Hey, sinner, you will become a saint. Why? Because of the covenant, the Lord is with you. Not because of what you're going to do; it's because of what He is going to do on behalf of you.

You know what is amazing; when you look into the Bible, Genesis 15, we all know that God and Abraham are having a conversation, and it starts with, 'After these things,' and I think about after what things? Genesis 14, Lot is captivated, Abraham takes 318 men (Genesis 14:14), fights the battle, rescues Lots, and gives everything. But something happens; suddenly Melchizedek appears; the high priest Melchizedek comes in; the king of Salem comes in; the king of righteousness comes in; and when he comes in, the Bible says, 'He gave Abraham the bread and wine.' Interesting! Abraham was not praying, Abraham was not fasting; Abraham was actually in a war; he won the battle; he came from there, and as he began to go back to his home, the king of Salem met him and gave him bread and wine. What did the king of Salem come and confirm to him? He said, 'Abraham, I am your portion.' Bread and Wine, he gave it to him, and then Abraham gave him tithes, and then something happened; the Bible says, 'After these things, God spoke to Abraham, and God entered into a covenant on behalf of Abraham.' The Bible declares in

Genesis 15, 'God gave a deep sleep to Abraham after giving him instructions to cut the animals; he laid them down; he cut all the animals but did not cut the birds and laid them, and Abraham understood that God was getting ready to get into a blood covenant.' Abraham expected that he and God were going to walk, but the Bible declares that God told Abraham, 'Okay, you take a

break, sleep. While Jesus on behalf of you will walk,' and we see that two things appear there, 'a smoking furnace and a burning lamp,' and these two things are representative of God the Father and God the Son, Jesus Christ, that they both walked into it on behalf of Abraham in that blood and they disappeared after that, and what we see is Abraham enjoying the benefits of it.

What were the benefits of it? God said to Abraham, 'Fear not Abraham, I am your shield an exceeding great reward.' So, God said to Abraham, Abraham, I'm going to protect you from everyone, and then not only that, I'm going to be your exceeding great reward that I'm going to magnify your name, I'm going to bless you with many blessings, everything that we see in Genesis 12 through 17, all the blessings that are promised to Abraham are going to come to pass because of the Covenant. Abraham asked God, 'God, You have promised me all these things, but what is the surety that you're going to make these things come to pass?' God said, 'You want surety; here is a surety, the Blood Covenant.' See the Blood Covenant, and that is the guarantee that every word that I speak to you will come to pass.

Now look at this; something unusual and amazing happens as the Father and the Son walk in that Blood Covenant. I almost imagine the Father looking at Jesus and saying, 'Son, 'If I fail to be loyal to Abraham and his race, then may this happen to me what happened to these animals; and Jesus saying to the Father, Father, if ever Abraham or his race fails to walk in your ways, may this happen to me what happened to these animals. Do you see what that blood covenant was about? It was not that Jesus said to the Father, If I ever fail You, may this happen to me. Jesus said to the Father, If ever mankind fails You, may this happen to me what happened to these animals. That was the power of the Blood Covenant! And so according to the promise, when Abraham's generation failed God when the mankind continued to commit sin and walk outside the will of the Lord.

Why did God give the Law when He was already in the covenant with His people?

The law was not for the strangers but was given as a product of that Covenant for God's own people; God did not give law to anybody in the world; God only gave the

law to Abraham's descendant, the Jewish people. Why? Because it was the product of the Covenant, and when God brought that Covenant and the law, the law revealed how sinful we were and how we failed God, but when we failed God, the consequences did not come upon you and me; the consequences came upon when Jesus walked with the Father on that blood. He said, 'Father, if ever mankind fails You, may this happen to me that happened to these animals, may my body be cut through.' And so, in the right time, Jesus came in the flesh. He said, 'Think not that I've come to abolish the law,' meaning I didn't come to undo the Covenant; I have come to fulfill the Covenant. (Mathew 5:17) What was the Covenant? To die, so that my body be broken, and one day He took the bread, and He said in, 'Luke 22:19 And he took bread, gave thanks and broke it, and gave it to them, saying, "This is my body given for you; do this in remembrance of me." Verse 20 goes on to tell us, 'In the same way, after the supper he took the cup, saying, "This cup is the new covenant in my blood, which is poured out for you. Why is your body broken for me Jesus? The simple answer is, I made a covenant with the Father on behalf of you that the day you fail, 'Father, may it happen to my body, as it is happening to these animals.' It's sealed us eternally, my friend. Our consequences were taken by Jesus Christ.

Let me tell you something else: God also, in Genesis 17 said, 'Hey listen, from now on this will be a sign for you as well that every Jewish boy who is born will be circumcised on the eighth day, and that will be a sign of my covenant with you and your generation.' Wow! So, every boy in his body carried a visible sign of God's covenant. Fast forward to many years, in 1 Samuel chapter 17 we see, one day, Goliath comes against Israel, and he begins to mock the armies of the Living God. Everybody is scared, and a Jewish boy comes running there. He brings food for his brothers and listens to what Goliath is saying, but suddenly he is not listening to what Goliath is saying; he does not see the stature of Goliath, but he's looking at, 'Am I not in Covenant with God?' How dare this man defies the army of the Living God wherein I bear the mark of Covenant on my body. Fast forward to Esther's time in book of Esther 4:16 we can see. Esther is scared. She says, 'If I perish, I perish. You all fast and pray; everybody fast and pray'. Why fasting? How is it that David did not even pray when he went to fight Goliath and

Esther is so terrified? The answer is she had forgotten that they were people in covenant with most high God. I want you to understand that David put his confidence in the Covenant that God made. He fully knew covenant meant God would fight my battles.

Now fast forward to the New Testament. Jesus said in Mathew 26:28, 'This is my blood of the new covenant.' As I began to study the word, I said, 'Lord, what is the difference between the New Covenant that You made versus the Covenant that You made with Abraham or all the other expressions of the Covenants we have in the Old Testament?' Let me tell you quickly, all other Covenant dealt with external enemies. The New Covenant deals with the external as well as the internal heart; it changes you. All other covenants were about doing. The New Covenant is about becoming.

The New Blood Covenant promises remission of sins.

Something so unusual and incredible happens when Jesus introduces His new blood covenant in Luke 22, and then Paul talks about it in 1 Corinthians 11:25 onwards. You begin to see that He says, 'This is the new covenant in my blood.' And in the new covenant, He says, 'There are remissions of your sin.' Something incredible: in the Old Covenant, the sins were covered for a period of a year; in the New Covenant, sin is dealt with permanently. In the Old Covenant, every year, there was a reminder of my sin when, during the Passover time, I would bring my sacrifice, but under the New Covenant, there is no more sacrifice needed; one sacrifice that happened finished it all forever. In the history of sacrifices, whenever a sacrifice would be happening, the fire would fall from heaven and consume the sacrifice once and for all, but one sacrifice happened in Jesus Christ when all the fire of heaven fell down, and the sacrifice didn't get consumed, but the sacrifice consumed the fire. That sacrifice is on behalf of you and me. Permanently dealt with. The Bible says, Hebrews 8:12, 'And I will forgive their wickedness, and I will never again remember their sins." None of the Old Testament covenants guarantee that. Only the New Covenant guarantees that. It's incredible!

The New Covenent; the Person & the Mind of Christ

Another very important thing that I've found about the New Covenant is that it changes my mind completely. Gives me ability to have access to mind of God. In Galatians 1:15 & 16, if you read it carefully, Paul is writing to the church in Galatians, and he says, 'It pleased the Father God to reveal His Son in me.' None of the Old Testament had the provision of God revealing His Son in us. God was releasing His blessings on behalf of us. He was dealing with our enemies externally, but He was not revealing His Son in us; He was becoming Emmanuel, but He was not coming on a residential visa to me. But the New Covenant promises something so beautiful: that now something else can happen because of the blood sacrifice of Jesus Christ, which is much bigger than what happened in Genesis 15, that God comes to stay in you and me. Hallelujah! Not only does He come and stay as a dormant person, He doesn't come and stay as a guest, He doesn't come and stay as a timid person, but the Bible declares that He is revealed in me. So, that simply means, if anybody wants a revelation of Christ, where to go? Paul said it in this way in 2 Corinthians 2:2-3, 'You yourselves are our letter, written on our hearts, known and read by everyone. You show that you are a letter from Christ, the result of our ministry, written not with ink but with the Spirit of the living God, not on tablets of stone but on tablets of human hearts.

Do you know one thing: the last letters of Jesus Christ are not found in book of Revelation? The last letters are you and me. We are the living letters given to the world, We are His story which Jesus is writing with His blood, that our lives have become living letters for the world to see because Christ is revealed in you and me. People who don't know Jesus can meet you and say, 'I see Jesus when I saw you, I see Jesus when I heard you, I see Jesus when you touched my life, Jesus touched my life, why? The answer is: Christ, His son, is revealed in me.

Paul says something incredible: he says, Christ, His son is revealed in me so that I may preach the gospel to the Gentiles. Wow! Do you know what the enemy tells you? He says, Look at your word, look at your thinking, look at how you talk, look at what you have done, look at your works. Do you really think God will use you, Paul? Look at

yourself. You persecuted the church. You killed so many. You took letters against churches. You persecuted people. You really think God is going to use you? **Hey, my history is not the premise of God using me; God uses me because Christ is revealed in me.** What I have done and what I have not done has nothing to do with this equation; Christ is sufficient who is in me. Hallelujah! Hallelujah! The New Covenant promises us that we can live from Christ in us.

Do you know that the Bible says in Colossians 1:27, '... Christ in me is the hope of glory.' It doesn't say Christ for me is the hope of glory; it doesn't say Christ with me is the hope of glory; it says Christ within me is the hope of glory. Our problem is that when we go through guilt and shame, condemnation and live focused on our mistakes we look for validation from people. Hey, stop doing that; look to Christ in you. The moment you begin to behold Christ in you, your life will never be the same again. Amen!

Christ in me was not promised in any of the Old Covenants; the New Covenant promises the Creator now staying in me. Paul says to the Church of Galatians. In Galatians 4:19, I labor so that Christ be formed in you. That Christ which is formed in me is also formed in you, and that is the sole purpose for which we as the New Covenant ministers stand and preach the good news. Why? So that Christ be formed in you, we don't come here to give you an intelligent argument about theology. Our goal is, Lord, when I preach, let Christ be formed in them! You know, God's desire and your willing submission to His willingness will give you all the benefits in His Covenant are your portion.

The Bible declares that, Christ in me is the will of the Father. Jesus said it in this way: in John 14:20 and 17:23 and many more scripture passages, He said, 'Father, as I am in You and they are in me, let them be one.' Wow! Jesus is saying, You in me and I in the Father. Now imagine that you and I are in Jesus Christ, and Jesus Christ is in the Father. So, question: Where are you? I am in Jesus, Jesus in the Father, so where am I? Father! Jesus is saying, who is saying? Jesus! Can Jesus speak lies? We know it is impossible for Him to speak lies. He is saying: 'You are in me and I am in the Father;

therefore, you are in the Father.' Now listen, friends, Old covenants do not give us this privilege; only the blood covenant in Jesus Christ marks our life for eternity in Him.

Now that also means something incredible. Let me tell you, if I am in Jesus and Jesus is in the Father, so if sickness has to touch me, before it touches me, who should it touch? So, if a curse has to touch me, who should it touch? If witchcraft has to touch me, who should it touch? If Lucifer has to touch me, who should he touch? If the devil has to touch me, who should he touch? And the answer: Buddy, he can never touch you! Some people are crazy; I don't know who taught that. I'm so sorry about it—the church is so messed up with spiritual warfare. So many people here asked me, 'Pastor, you come from India, so heavy there. How's this happening? How's that happening there? ' I said, How crazy that is. You're telling Jesus Christ you came on earth, so heavy here, how can you operate? You read about the wrong Jesus; change how you read your Bible. Listen, Jesus is not scared of darkness; darkness is scared of Jesus! So, what did Apostle Paul teach to the church in Galatia? Look at Galatians 3:27 (NLT) And all who have been united with Christ in baptism have put on Christ, like putting on new clothes. What do you think this means? This simply mean, I am covered with Christ, top to bottom. Colossians 3:3 says, 'We died, and our life is hidden in Jesus Christ.' It's not promised in the Old Covenants. Abraham, sorry you didn't have this privilege; I have this. You are the father of Faith; fantastic. But I have something you didn't have! David, you didn't have something that I have. None of the Old Testament guys have anything that we have. You know, when we go to heaven, I think they will come running to us and say, Hey, tell me one thing: how is it to have God in you? He just came upon us, and we saw great miracles, including the Red Sea divided. What does it mean when He is in you? You're not going to go look for Moses; Moses is going to come looking for you because the Bible says they meaning all the heroes of old testament were looking for this and they wanted this, but God gave it to us.

Hallelujah! We are not second-class citizens in the kingdom of God who are trying to battle and somehow manage to enter. Let me tell you something: most people think that the promised land is the Kingdom of God. No friends! Promised land is nowhere the Kingdom of God. In the promised land, there were giants. In the Kingdom of God,

there are no giants. Don't worry about them. Something incredible the Bible says in 1 John 4:4, 'Greater is He who is in you than he who is in the world.' Once a missionary met me here and said, Pastor, I'm going and serving in the darkest place. Would you pray for me that angels would be released? I said, Have you gone mad? Angel needs your help; you don't need their help. Why? Because you are greater than angels, what's wrong with you? 'Angels, you stand in front of me, behind me,' that is Psalm 91 for old Covenant people; my Covenant is better than Psalm 91. Do you really know that? 'Oh Angel, protect those who are righteous.' I don't need angelic protection when the Elohim is in me. In fact, do you know what? Angels wait for the Revelation that I preach so that they can do what they are supposed to do. Taking the help of an angel to protect you is a demotion for the church because you don't know who you are. Look at Jesus in the garden of Gethsemane when the Roman soldiers came to arrest Him, He refused to take Angelic protection. He said that if I call Angels they will come and aid me, but all He had to say was, I AM' when they asked Him who is Jesus? What happened as a result all fell down to the ground Apostle John in his gospel recorded it for us, John 18:6. If you only know what Jesus knew, the scariest place in the world would become the most delightsome playground for you.

## The New Blood covenant, Divine Nature and One Spirit with God!

In II Peter 1:4, another great provision of the new blood covenant is that we become the partakers of divine nature. Abraham the Covenant with you was protection and providence but not character change. But the covenant with me is that I no longer live; Christ lives in me. My nature is gone; I have put on a new man. Old things are gone; I become a new creation. By the way, do you know that the new creation means it has no history? 'New' means it never existed before. If it existed before, it would be modification, not new, but the Bible says He has made us New Creation. You know when Apostles put this word 'New Creation.' Why? Because we have no reference for it. Heavens had no grid for the new creation, and that's what God made you and me. This new creation is an exact replica of Jesus Christ. So much so that the Bible says in

1 Corinthians 6:17, that we are those who fellowship with the Lord and become one spirit with Him. Now think about it: the day I become born again, I used to think, Jesus's Spirit is in me and my spirit is in me, so I have two spirits in me. Like David said, 'Cast me not away from your presence, oh Lord, and

do not let Your Spirit forsake me.' David, that was a possibility for you, but for me, that's not a possibility. Why? because in the New Covenant, Jesus said, He will come and abide with me forever. David had a fear of losing the Holy Spirit; I don't. Why? It's sealed in the Blood Covenant of Jesus Christ. So, if we commit sin, don't think the Holy Spirit leaves; just know now that when we fall or commit sin, He comes and empowers us and picks us up, puts us back on track and says, 'Come on, boy, run again!'

We are not supposed to have a weak, defeated life. We with the Spirit of the Lord are more than over-comers. Do you know one thing? We don't have to enter the battle; the battle is already won; Jesus has won it for us, and you and I become more than over- comers. Abraham did not have this privilege; you and I have this privilege. We are more than over-comers at all times, at all places, in every circumstance. There is nothing changing that; the blood of Jesus has sealed it for us. It is incredible truth. We become one spirit with Jesus. 1 Corinthians 6:17 & 1 Corinthians 2:16: 'Not only have I become one spirit with Jesus, I have the mind of Christ. Woohoo! The New Covenant tells you, son, that this mind, which is the result of the fruit that Adam ate of the tree of knowledge of good and evil, is done away with when I give you the mind of Christ. You have Jesus' mind, and Jesus' mind is so crazy everybody tells Lazarus is dead. He said, No, he's sleeping. Next thing, the Bible declares, not only my spirit is one with Christ, not only my mind is one with Christ. I have the mind of Christ; something incredible happens in 1 Corinthians 12:27 'I am the body of Christ.' The New Covenant is incredible! Old Covenant, Abraham, I will fight your battles, I will bless those who bless you, and all those external blessings are yours, but in the New Covenant your body becomes my body, says Jesus. No wonder when I lay hands on sick, sick recovers. Why? Because it's the body of Christ. Therefore, the Bible says, glorify God in your bodies. Hallelujah! My friend, I want you to know this: the only way we put our body to shame is because we identify with the old nature, which is no longer alive. It's just in our heads & old habits, we are deceived by the lies of the enemy saying, 'That's who you are,' no, my friend! You are what Jesus said in the New Covenant, and the moment you realize that, sin habits are broken, Like a thread in a fire, so is sin addiction in the presence of God. When He comes and invades your spirit, soul, and body, your life is never the same again.

**The blood of New Covenent and co-crucification!**

Another incredible thing that I have seen is Galatians 6:14, where Paul said, 'I am crucified to the world on the cross, and the world is crucified to me on the cross. Listen, what does that mean? That means I am done away with the world and its system, and the world is done away with me and my system. I no longer belong to the world; I belong to Heaven. Listen, I am no longer just for heaven; I am from heaven because Jesus came from the Father to do the will of the Father, so you and I are on this earth to do the will of the Father and one day head home. Isn't it incredible that the New Covenant said, 'Where I stay, you will stay also.' I'll come to take you so that you will stay where I stay. It's beautiful, my friend. There is nothing that the New Covenant doesn't give us that is given to Jesus. Everything that Jesus had is ours. Galatians 2:20 says, 'I no longer live; Christ lives in me.' Paul, what do you mean by that? Simple answer: I live from the reality of the New Covenant.

**The blood of New Covenent and The Bride!**

Another thing it says, Only the New Covenant makes you and I into a bride of Jesus Christ. Think about it. Abraham, God entered into a covenant on behalf of you, but you were not made the bride of Christ. The New Covenant, the Blood, He purchased us with the Blood so that He can present us as a chest virgin to Him.

Ephesians 5:25-27, 'Husbands, love your wives, just as Christ loved the church and gave himself up for her to make her holy, cleansing her by the washing with water through the word, and to present her to himself as a radiant church, without stain or wrinkle or any other blemish, but holy and blameless.

## The Blood Covenent & The table of the Lord!

I want to give you this word of encouragement: when you break the bread and when you take the wine, does it remind you like Adam's body was broken open and God took a rib out of him and gave him a women and when he looked at his wife for the first time and said, bone of my bone and flesh of my flesh, Similarly on the cross Jesus' body was broken open and what came out as a result was His Bride. Jesus said, 'This is my new blood covenant for you.' Not just for the forgiveness of sin, but to actually make you my own. So, today we have a choice to believe this gospel.

## The Old Covenant and Its Limitations:

Under the Old Covenant, God established a system of laws, sacrifices, and rituals to address sin and provide a way for humanity to approach Him. The Mosaic

Covenant, delivered to Israel at Mount Sinai, was based on obedience to the law and the shedding of animal blood as atonement for sins.

1. A Temporary Covering for Sin:
- Leviticus 17:11: "For the life of a creature is in the blood, and I have given it to you to make atonement for yourselves on the altar; it is the blood that makes atonement for one's life."
- Animal sacrifices temporarily covered sin but could not remove its guilt or cleanse the conscience.
- Example: The annual Day of Atonement (Yom Kippur) involved the high priest offering sacrifices to atone for the sins of the nation. However, this had to be repeated every year (Hebrews 10:1-4).

2. Limited Access to God:
- The presence of God was confined to the Holy of Holies,

which only the high priest could enter once a year (Exodus 26:33-34; Hebrews 9:7).
- The law exposed sin but could not transform the heart (Romans 3:20). II. The New Covenant in the Blood of Jesus
- Jesus declared, "This is my blood of the covenant, which is poured out for many for the forgiveness of sins" (Matthew 26:28). His blood established a better covenant, fulfilling the Old Covenant and surpassing it in every way.

1. Redemption and Forgiveness:
- Ephesians 1:7 "In Him, we have redemption through His blood, the forgiveness of sins, according to the riches of His grace."
- Unlike the blood of animals, which could only cover sin temporarily, the blood of Jesus removes sin completely (Hebrews 10:10-12).
- Example: When Jesus cried, "It is finished!" (John 19:30), He signified the ultimate payment for sin had been made.

2. Cleansing and Purification:
- 1 John 1:7: "The blood of Jesus, His Son, purifies us from all sin."
- Hebrews 9:14: "How much more will the blood of Christ... cleanse our consciences from acts that lead to death."
- The Old Covenant could not cleanse the inner man, but the blood of Jesus purifies the heart and conscience, enabling believers to serve God in holiness.

3. Justification:
- Romans 5:9: "Since we have now been justified by His blood, how much more shall we be saved from God's wrath through Him!"
- Justification means being declared righteous before God. Under the New Covenant, believers are not only forgiven but also counted as righteous through the blood of Jesus (2 Corinthians 5:21).

4. Reconciliation:
- Colossians 1:20: "And through Him to reconcile to Himself all things, whether things on earth or things in heaven, by making peace through His blood, shed on the cross."
- The Old Covenant highlighted humanity's separation from God; the New Covenant restores peace and fellowship with Him.

5. Sanctification:
- Hebrews 13:12: "Jesus also suffered outside the city gate to make the people holy through His own blood."
- Sanctification involves being set apart for God. The blood of Jesus makes believers holy, a process the Old Covenant could not fully accomplish.

6. Victory Over Satan:
- Revelation 12:11: "They triumphed over him by the blood of the Lamb and by the word of their testimony."
- The blood of Jesus disarms Satan's accusations, securing victory for believers.

7. Eternal Life and the New Covenant:
- Hebrews 9:15: "For this reason Christ is the mediator of a new covenant, that those who are called may receive the promised eternal inheritance."
- The New Covenant is eternal, providing everlasting life and fellowship with God (John 3:16).

III. The Superiority of the New Covenant

1. Fulfillment of the Old Covenant:
- Matthew 5:17: Jesus said, "Do not think that I have come to abolish the Law or the Prophets; I have not come to abolish them but to fulfill them."
- Every requirement of the Old Covenant—its laws, sacrifices, and priesthood—was perfectly fulfilled in Jesus.

2. A Better Sacrifice:
- Hebrews 9:12: "He did not enter by means of the blood of

goats and calves; but He entered the Most Holy Place once for all by His own blood, thus obtaining eternal redemption."
- Jesus' sacrifice was once for all, unlike the repeated sacrifices of the Old Covenant.

3. Direct Access to God:
- Hebrews 10:19-22: "Therefore, brothers and sisters, since we have confidence to enter the Most Holy Place by the blood of Jesus, let us draw near to God with a sincere heart."
- Believers no longer need an earthly high priest or temple rituals; they have direct access to God through Jesus.

4. Transformation of the Heart:
- Jeremiah 31:33: "I will put my law in their minds and write it on their hearts."
- The New Covenant empowers believers to live in righteousness through the Holy Spirit (Ezekiel 36:26-27).

IV. Living in the Power of the Blood of Jesus

As believers, we are called to walk in the benefits of Christ's blood:

1. Confidence in Forgiveness: No condemnation for those in Christ (Romans 8:1).
2. Holiness: Living set apart for God through sanctification.
3. Victory: Overcoming sin and Satan by standing firm in the finished work of Christ.
4. Unity: The blood of Jesus unites all believers into one body (Ephesians 2:13-14).

*Righteousness in His Blood*

*The blood of Jesus establishes a covenant far superior to all others. It brings complete forgiveness, eternal reconciliation, and transformative power to those who believe. By the blood of Jesus, we are declared righteous, made holy, and given the assurance of eternal life. This New Covenant is the ultimate expression of God's grace and the foundation of our hope.*

*Let us continually rejoice in the blood of Jesus, which speaks a better word than the blood of Abel (Hebrews 12:24), and live as people made righteous by His sacrifice.*

## Chapter 14

# Righteousness and Judgment

Every man and woman will one day die, but death is not the end, death is merely the beginning. What follows after death is dictated by that which first occurs here on earth. In the same way that every person will face death, every person will also face judgment. No soul will escape the righteous judgment of God. Hebrews 9:27 (NLT) tells us, *"Each person is destined to die once, and after that, comes judgment."* Now, there are five pillars of judgment. Number one is how you have lived according to the law. Number two is what measure of love you have lived by. Number three is your holiness. Number four is your works. And number five is how you have utilized the opportunities given to you.

You will be judged based on how you have lived according to the law, because the law reveals to us what sin is. But my friend, you will fail, for we are told in James 2:10 that if you are lacking in even one piece of the law then you have been insufficient in all of it. You will be judged based on the measure you have loved, because the greatest commandments state, *"Love the Lord your God with all your heart, soul, mind, and strength, and love your neighbor as yourself"* (Mark 12:30-31 NLT). You will fail because everyone has been hurtful to a loved one, felt jealousy, acted harshly, and grieved the Spirit of God. John 14:15 explains that if you love the Lord, you will obey His commands, and we have all disobeyed our God at some point in our lives. You will be judged based on your holiness because it is written in 1 Peter that we are to be holy as He is holy. Again, you will fail because all have fallen short of the glory of God and have lived according to the flesh. You will be judged based on your works because Matthew 25:31 (TPT) onwards states,

> *"When the Son of Man comes in His glory, and all the angels with Him, then He will sit on His glorious throne. Before Him will be gathered all the nations,*

*and He will separate people one from another as a shepherd separates sheep from the goats. And He will separate the sheep on His right and the goats on His left. Then the King will say to those on His right, 'Come you who are blessed by my Father inherit the kingdom prepared for you from the foundations of the world. For I was hungry and you gave me food, I was thirsty and you gave me drink, I was a stranger and you welcomed me, I was naked and you clothed me, I was sick and you visited me, I was in prison and you came to me.' Then the righteous will answer Him saying, 'Lord, when did we see you hungry and feed you and thirsty and give you drink? And when did we see you as a stranger and welcome you, or naked and clothe you? And when did we see you sick or in prison and visit you?' And the king will answer them, 'Truly I say to you, as you did it to one of the least of these my brothers, you did it to me.' Then He will say to those on His left, depart from me, you cursed, into the eternal fire prepared for the devil and his angels. For I was hungry and you gave me no food, I was thirsty and you gave me no drink, I was a stranger and you did not welcome me, naked and you did not clothe me, sick and in prison and you did not visit me.'"*

No man can say that he was always generous and compassionate to those who had nothing to offer him. No man can say that he has never made a selfish decision, so again, you will fail. And this brings me to the last judgment: you will be judged on how you have utilized the opportunities given you because Luke 12:48 (NKJV) declares that, "*To whom much is given, much is required.*" And my friend, we have all, at some point, squandered an opportunity and so, here again, we will fail

Having acknowledged that we will not pass the test based on our records, I want to bring something to your attention. If your entry into heaven is based on the book of records, then my friend, you will not enter. But what if I told you that your entry into heaven had nothing at all to do with the book of records?

## The Book of Life and The Great White Throne

I would like you to understand a passage that will give you a clearer picture of judgment day. This passage is found in Revelation 20:11-15 (ESV).

> *"Then I saw a great white throne and Him who was seated on it. From His presence earth and sky fled away, and no place was found for them. And I saw the dead, great and small, standing before the throne and books were opened. Then another book was opened, which is the Book of Life. And the dead were judged by what was written in the books, according to what they had done. And the sea gave up the dead who were in it, death and Hades gave up the dead who were in them, and they were judged, each one of them according to what they had done. Then death and Hades were thrown into the lake of fire. This is the second death, the lake of fire. And if anyone's name was not found written in the Book of Life, he was thrown into the lake of fire."*

I want you to remember this title, *"The Great White Throne."* Now, there are a few major facts to note when reading this scripture; it reveals to us that when Jesus comes to judge, all will be judged great and small and none can flee nor hide. We are told that after judgment, death and Hades will be thrown into the lake of fire. And finally, and maybe most importantly, it is made known to us through this scripture that there are *books* that will be opened. In this, we know that there are more books than just the book of records, and in the last verse it states, *"If anyone's name was not found written in the Book of Life, he was thrown into the lake of fire."* The only book that ordains your entry into heaven is the Book of Life. The devil may use your record to inflict fear and shame, but your works, good or bad, are not the deciding factor when it comes to heaven or hell.

I want to emphasize the gravity of this fact. The only criteria that heaven requires is for your name to be written in the book of life. This brings us to another great matter, what does it take to have your name written in the Book of Life?

Luke 10:20 (NKJV) says, *"Nevertheless, do not rejoice in this, that the spirits are subjected to you, but rejoice that your names are written in heaven."* It is a common misconception within the church to believe that the attending of a church equates to salvation. Salvation is not acquired by works, it is a gift that is granted to those who cast their belief on the Son of God. Jesus explained in Matthew 7:22 that there will be people who, having no personal relationship with Christ, will profess to have cast out demons and done miracles in His name, and He will tell them, *"I do not know you."* This proves that signs and wonders are not the answer and do not dictate the validity of your salvation. There are those who argue theology and squabble about belief, claiming that an act such as baptism is the answer, but these are childish debates. It is time for the church to grow into maturity and move away from the foundational elements as Paul tells us in Hebrews six. Baptism is a beautiful expression of your belonging to Christ but it is not the seal of your salvation.

The man next to Jesus on the cross is a perfect example of the simplicity of the gift of salvation. A broken man recognizing his sin and turning to the savior in pure faith praying a simple request, *"Jesus, remember me when you come into your kingdom."* And Jesus, replying with a priceless promise, *"Truly, I say to you, today you will be with me in paradise."* Now, this man had no water baptism, miracle, or college degree to show for this. His record leading up to the very moment of his salvation would have failed every test, but this is what Jesus came to do. If a man who knew no sin could become sin, then a sinner can be made righteous. Christ has taken our sin that resembles crimson and scarlet and made it as white as snow. There are too many Christians living their entire life in fear of failing, in fear of falling shy of heaven. It is terrible to know that some of the most miserable people in the world are Christians. Like a bride who is paranoid unto sickness that her husband will leave her, is where much of the church is. In the past when we as Christians have heard scripture passages such as Revelation twenty-one verse eight listing sinners including cowards, murderers, liars, and the sexually immoral, we have made a big mistake. We instantly identify with the sins and sinners, and this has been a costly error for the Bride of Christ. It is a lie that your Father sees you as a sinner. It is a lie that our righteous Judge would send His redeemed ones into the lake of fire, and we must not live in fear of such deception! There is now no condemnation for those who are in Christ Jesus. This means that you will not be condemned on the day of judgment. Revelation 3:5 (ESV) assures us of a great thing, *"The one who conquers will be clothed in white garments, and I will never blot his name out of the book of life. I will confess his name before my Father and before His angels."* This is a promise from Jesus our savior. Heaven is awaiting the Bride; it is anticipating the bridal procession to celebrate Her, not to condemn Her. We are told in Proverbs 11:4 (TPT), *"When Judgment day comes, all the wealth of the world won't help you one bit. So be rich in righteousness, for that is the only thing that can save you in death."* The book of life is reserved for the righteous, and righteousness is established by belief in the Son.

> The book of life is reserved for the righteous, and righteousness is established by belief in the Son

It is, however, important that you understand that although the Church will not be condemned, as we are told in Romans 14:10 (NLT), *"So why do you condemn another believer? Why do you look down on another believer? Remember, we all stand before the judgment seat of God."* No believer will be condemned, but that does not mean that they will not be judged on the last day.

## The Judgment Seat of Christ

There are two places where judgment will commence. The first is *"The Great White Throne."* This is where the judgment of non-believers will take place. The Lord will separate the goats from the sheep and judge who will be sentenced to hell. *"And if anyone's name was not found written in the Book of Life, he was thrown into the lake of fire"* (Revelation 20:15 NLT). If you have been taught that the children of God and the goats will be judged together, then let me re-teach you. The Church will not be judged at The Great White Throne. When the world appears before The Great White Throne; we will not be standing beside the world. We might likely be sitting next to Jesus as fellow judges with Him!" There is another place of judgment and it is named, *"The Judgment seat of Christ."* This is where the Church will be judged, but it will not be deciphering who will go to heaven or hell. Remember that your name will never be blotted out from the Book of Life. *The Judgment seat of Christ will be about rewards and losses.*

Open your heart to a passage of scripture found in 1 Corinthians 3:10-15 (NIV).

> *"By the grace God has given me, I laid a foundation as a wise builder, and someone else is building on it. But each one should build with care, for no one can lay any foundation other than the one already laid, which is Jesus Christ. If anyone builds on this foundation using gold, silver, costly stones, wood, hay or straw, their work will be shown for what it is, because the Day will bring it to light. It will be revealed with fire, and the fire will test the quality of each person's work. If what has been built survives, the builder will receive a reward. If it is burned up, the builder will suffer loss, yet will still be saved-even though only as one escaping through the flames."*

I find it significant that stronger metals, such as iron or titanium, are not exemplified in these verses. Metals such as gold and silver, or precious stones and costly jewels, are desired based on value and rarity over strength. Gold and silver become further esteemed after being under the scrutiny of fire; they are made pure in the flames. In this we know that there are things in this life that hold value in the eyes of the Lord, and this is what is going to be tested at the Judgment seat of Christ. If you are basing your life on feelings and fleshly tendencies, and laying your foundation with selfishness and fading achievements, be assured that it will crumble into flames. Every thought, action, and word will be tested on that day, and anything that is not of Jesus will not make it. I want you to know exactly what it is that will not burn away in the fire; I want you to know where the eternal gold is hidden and how to extract it. My friend, every treasure, every crown, and every eternal valuable is found in the pages of the Word of God. It is important that you also note that our eternal treasure is not based on our *good works*. Even some of the unbelievers I know live their life with high morals and kind gestures, but this is not what will grant you a crown. The crowns of heaven are of immense eternal value, but can only be earned in this life. Honor in heaven is based on the crowns that you have secured here on earth, and you do not earn crowns by *being good*, but rather by walking in the promises of God.

**The Crowns**

Psalms 8:4 (ESV) reads, *"What is man that you are mindful of him, and you have crowned him with glory and honor."* This verse reveals that when God created Adam He placed a crown of glory and honor upon his head. Adam wore this crown until the day that the devil deceived him, and when Adam bowed to Satan, his crown fell at the feet of the enemy. In that moment, Satan did not only steal the crown of glory and honor from Adam, but he stole it from all of humanity. Even after this great fall and this terrible devastation of mankind, God never gave up on Adam and He never gave up on humanity. God had devised a plan for redemption, and Jesus came to earth. Jesus did not come with a crown like Adam did; He was born with every obstacle that has cursed the fallen man. Jesus came to earth as an empty vessel, and yet He ascended from the earth with every crown that will never fade. All that Jesus was given was the Word of God; He was given every promise from His Father, and that was enough to conquer Satan and take back every crown that was once lost.

There are seven times that crowns are mentioned in the Bible that I would like to explore. I want you to understand that even Jesus did not come wearing a crown, meaning that these crowns are not our birth-right. But each believer is given the means to acquire and earn every crown mentioned in the Word of God.

The first is *'the crown of life'*. This crown is mentioned twice, the first being in James 1:12 (NKJV). *"Blessed is the man who endures temptation; for when he has been approved, he will receive the crown of life which the Lord has promised to those who love Him."* The crown of life that is found in James is for the faithful. This crown is bestowed upon those who remain faithful to the Lord during temptation, it is reserved for the ones who love and obey the Lord in the battle against the flesh.

The crown of life is mentioned a second time in Revelation 2:10 (NKJV); this is also known as 'The Crown of Martyrs.' *"Do not fear any of those things that you are about to suffer. Indeed, the devil is about to throw some of you in prison, that you may be tested, and you will have tribulation ten days. Be faithful until death, and I will give you the crown of life."* This is The Crown of Martyrs, and it will be granted to those who have endured hardship and persecution and have been faithful to the end.

The third Crown is the imperishable crown; this is the crown of discipline and integrity that is mentioned in 1 Corinthians 9:24-27 (NKJV).

> *"Do you not know that those who run in a race all run, but one receives the prize? Run in such a way that you may obtain it. And everyone who competes is temperate in all things. Now, they do it to obtain a perishable crown, but we for an imperishable crown. Therefore I run: not with uncertainty. Therefore I fight: not as one who beats the air. But I discipline my body*

*and bring it into subjection, lest when I have preached to others, I myself should become disqualified."*

Paul says that everyone may run, but not everyone will win the prize. This crown is reserved for those who discipline their bodies and minds and bring them into alignment with their spirit. This crown is not for those who preach one thing but live another. This crown is only for those who possess integrity and authenticity, who cling to that which is eternal, and who live their lives running after a prize that is imperishable and everlasting!

The fourth crown is The Crown of Rejoicing! You will find this crown in 1 Thessalonians 2:19 (NKJV). *"For what is our hope, or our joy, or our crown of rejoicing? Is it not even you in the presence of our Lord Jesus Christ at His coming? For you are our glory and joy."* This is the crown of souls, friends and family, people who you evangelize to, people you lead out of the darkness! The brothers and sisters you disciple; the ones who you love and cherish with the love of Jesus Christ. This is the great commission; was it not to reach and save the lost? The harvest is ready! People! People! People will be your crown on that day; people are your crown of rejoicing!

The fifth crown is The Crown of Righteousness. In 2 Timothy 4:6-8 (NKJV) Paul writes one of his last letters in the face of death,

> *"For I am already being poured out as a drink offering, and the time of my departure is at hand. I have fought the good fight, I have finished the race, I have kept the faith. Finally, there is laid up for me the crown of righteousness, which the Lord, the righteous Judge, will give to me on that day, and not to me only, but also to all who have loved His appearing."*

The crown of righteousness is for those who use their opportunities to glorify the Lord. This crown will be given to the ones who abide in the Spirit and the Word, those who have been a vessel for Jesus, a ripple of His life and gospel! Those who receive this crown will be bold on the day of His coming because they are the ones who love His appearing. Hallelujah!

The sixth crown is The Crown of Glory. The Crown of Glory is found in First Peter 5:1-4 (NKJV).

> *"The elders who are among you I exhort, I who am a fellow elder and a witness of the sufferings of Christ, and also a partaker of the glory that will be revealed: Shepherd the flock of God which is among you, serving as overseers, not by compulsion but willingly, not for dishonest gain but eagerly; nor as being lords over those entrusted to you but being examples to the flock; and when the Chief Shepherd appears, you will receive the Crown of Glory that does not fade away."*

This crown is laid aside for the wholehearted servants of the Body of Christ. Those who lead by serving; love by sacrificing; grow by deepening their roots, they *will* be glorified at the Judgment seat of Christ. It doesn't matter if you are the pastor or on the clean up crew, if you serve wholeheartedly and if you do it for the Lord, then you will never go unnoticed and on the last day, Jesus will crown you with the Crown of Glory!

The seventh crown mentioned in the Bible is found in Revelation 3:11(TPT). This verse reveals something very important. *"But I come swiftly, so cling tightly to what you have, so that no one may seize your crown of victory."* In this we know that there are things in this world that will try to snatch the crown from your hands. There are distractions, traps, and hindrances, and if you let yourself wander or lose focus it may cost you something very dear. We are being warned in this verse to cling to Jesus and to the gifts and fruit He is growing in our lives. Do not wander or live recklessly; do not waste your life or act foolishly, cling with all you have to the Son; fight with all your strength to keep your gaze fastened on the blessed savior, and you will not lose your crown of victory!

I want you to know one more incredible thing about Judgment Day. In First Corinthians 6:3 (TPT) we are told,

> *"Don't you realize that we, the Holy ones, will judge the universe? If the unbelieving world is under your jurisdiction, you should be fully competent to settle these trivial lawsuits among yourselves. For surely you know that we will one day judge angels, let alone these everyday matters."*

When the world appears before The Great White Throne; we will not be standing beside the world, we will be sitting next to Jesus as fellow judges with Him. You may recall in the scripture where it tells us that Jesus comes with thousands of Holy Ones, including you and I, and all of creation is anticipating that day! The day is coming when all will be judged, when books will be opened, and nothing will be hidden. The day is coming when the world will stand before The Great White Throne, and all who did not believe will be cast away. The day is coming when every believer will appear before The Judgment Seat of Christ, and all they have built will be tested and tried by fire; there will be rewards and losses on that day. My friend, I want you to understand that you will be bold on that day if you chase after Jesus and love His promises and Word. I want you to begin to build with precious metals and stones, to cling to that which has eternal value. We are told in Matthew 6:19-21 (ESV),

> *"Do not lay up for yourselves treasures on earth, where moth and rust destroy and where thieves break in and steal; but lay up for yourselves treasures in heaven, where neither moth nor rust destroys, and where thieves do not break in and steal. For where your treasure is, there also your heart will be."*

My prayer is that there would be no more wasted Christians; that there would be no more Christians whose lives do not reflect Christ, who live only for themselves and for the things that are fleeting. No more Christians who love the Spirit of Christ but revile His Body, or who love His Body but neglect His spirit;

who make it to heaven but only as through a wall of fire! I pray for Christians to awaken and arise in their identities and callings. I pray for Believers who live from a place of conviction and discernment. I desire to see God's people heaven-conscious and not self-conscious. All of creation desperately desires God's children to step into their authority and take back every crown that was stolen from Adam. Jesus has made the way straight, He has fulfilled every law, attained every crown, and He has done it for you! Righteousness is not something that is far off and out of reach, righteousness is right standing with God. It is living with a goal of one thing... Jesus!

Jesus is the goal! When you live a life established in righteousness, you will face judgment day like you have faced every day on earth, as bold as a lion and in love with the appearing of Christ Jesus! Hallelujah, amen!

Bijapur, Chattisgarh

Nandurbar, Maharashtra

Pune, Maharashtra

Vyara, Gujarat

Vyara, Gujarat

Katihar, Bihar

Nagpur, Maharashtra

New Delhi

Dallas Texas, USA

Joshua & Mae David

# Joshua Barnabas David

## Joshua Barnabas David

### For Indian Donors

Bank Name: **American National Bank of Texas**
Address: 1101 E Plano Pkwy, Plano, TX 75074
Routing: 111901519
Account #: 4601043146

**Kingdom Builders Global**
Type: 501C3
EIN: 99-4771326
Address: 2221 High Country Dr, Carrollton, TX 75007
Checks: Make Payable to "Kingdom Builders Global"

PayPal
kingdombuildersglobalinc@gmail.com

**Other ways to donate**

# Other ways to donate

KingdomBuildersGlobalinc@gmail.com

www.ingramcontent.com/pod-product-compliance
Lightning Source LLC
Chambersburg PA
CBHW071116160426
43196CB00013B/2591